FOOD&WINE
COCKTAILS
2016

FOOD & WINE COCKTAILS 2016
EXECUTIVE EDITOR **Kate Krader**
CHIEF MIXOLOGIST **John deBary**
EDITOR **Susan Choung**
COPY EDITOR **Lisa Leventer**
EDITORIAL ASSISTANT **Kate Malczewski**
RESEARCHER **Ryan Harrington**
TEST KITCHEN ASSISTANT **Emily Tylman**

CREATIVE DIRECTOR **Fredrika Stjärne**
ART DIRECTOR **James Maikowski**
PHOTO EDITOR **Sara Parks**
DESIGNER **Alisha Petro**
PRODUCTION DIRECTOR **Joseph Colucci**
PRODUCTION MANAGERS **Stephanie Thompson,
 David Richey**

PRINCIPAL PHOTOGRAPHY
 (INCLUDING FRONT AND BACK COVERS)
PHOTOGRAPHER **David Malosh**
STYLIST **Adrienne Anderson**
For additional photo contributors, see p. 217.

ON THE COVER **Bourbon Chai Milk Punch, p. 65**

Copyright © 2016 Time Inc. Books

Published by Time Inc. Books
225 Liberty Street
New York, NY 10281

FOOD & WINE is a trademark of Time Inc. Affluent Media
Group, registered in the U.S. and other countries.

ISBN-10: 0-8487-4839-5

ISBN-13: 978-0-8487-4839-5

ISSN 1554-4354

Manufactured in the United States of America

FOOD&WINE
COCKTAILS
2016

FOOD&WINE
BOOKS

CONTENTS

FLAVOR KEY

These symbols tell what to expect in each drink.

- ● **STRONG** High alcohol content by volume
- ● **SWEET** Simple syrup, honey, sweet liqueurs or mixers
- ● **TART** Lemon, lime or other citrus
- ● **BITTER** Bitters, Campari or other bitter liqueurs
- ● **FRUITY** Berries, melons, other fruit or fruit-based liqueurs
- ● **HERBAL** Herbs, Chartreuse or other herbal liqueurs
- ● **SMOKY** Mezcal, peated Scotch or other smoky ingredients
- ● **SPICY** Chiles, cayenne, ginger or other hot ingredients

FOREWORD

Not long ago, a bar with a slushie machine wasn't the place to go for an interesting cocktail. Now, bartenders are redeeming frozen drinks by using high-quality spirits and fresh juices. This is just one of the fun and inspiring trends we're highlighting in *F&W Cocktails 2016*, with recipes from 40 of the country's top mixologists. These trends cover the spectrum, from low-proof drinks that take advantage of terrific aperitifs to high-octane cocktails such as Desk Job (p. 116), which tastes like a powerful, complex rum and Coke. Then there are those slushie drinks, like a frozen piña colada made with excellent rum and coconut water (p. 90). So not only can you proudly drink your slushie at a bar, you can also easily make one in your blender at home.

Kate Krader
Executive Editor
FOOD & WINE Cocktails

John deBary
Chief Mixologist
FOOD & WINE Cocktails 2016

GLASSWARE

1 MARTINI

A stemmed glass with a cone-shaped bowl for cocktails served straight up (mixed with ice and then strained).

2 ROCKS

A short, wide-mouthed glass for spirits served neat (without ice) and cocktails poured over ice. **Single rocks** glasses hold 6 to 8 ounces; **double rocks** glasses hold 12 to 14 ounces.

3 COLLINS

A very tall, narrow glass often used for drinks that are served on ice and topped with soda.

4 WINEGLASS

A tall, slightly rounded, stemmed glass for wine-based cocktails. White wine glasses are a fine substitute for highball glasses and are also a good choice for frozen drinks. Balloon-shaped red wine glasses are ideal for fruity cocktails as well as punches.

5 HIGHBALL

A tall, narrow glass for cocktails that are served with ice and topped with sparkling beverages such as club soda, tonic water or ginger beer.

6 COUPE

A shallow, wide-mouthed, stemmed glass primarily for small (short) and potent cocktails that are served straight up. Although the coupe was originally designed to hold Champagne, its shape is more decorative than functional. Most coupes have a capacity of 4 to 8 ounces.

7 PILSNER

A tall, flared glass designed for beer. It's also good for oversize cocktails on ice, drinks with multiple garnishes or as a substitute for a tiki mug.

8 HEATPROOF GLASS OR MUG

A durable ceramic or glass cup with a handle. Perfect for coffee spiked with whiskey or other spirits as well as toddies and other hot drinks.

9 FLUTE

A tall, slender, usually stemmed glass; its narrow shape helps keep Champagne or sparkling wine cocktails effervescent.

10 JULEP CUP

A short metal cup designed to keep juleps (minty, crushed-ice cocktails) cold. Julep cups are traditionally silver but these days can be found in copper or stainless steel.

11 FIZZ

A narrow glass for soda-topped drinks without ice. Also called a juice glass or Delmonico glass.

12 TIKI MUG

A tall sculptural mug, usually without a handle, that's decorated with a Polynesian-style or tropical motif.

SNIFTER (not pictured)

A wide-bowled glass for spirits served neat or potent cocktails.

BAR TOOLS

1 HAWTHORNE STRAINER

The best all-purpose strainer. A semicircular spring ensures a spill-proof fit on a shaker. Look for a tightly coiled spring, which keeps muddled fruit and herbs out of drinks.

2 JIGGER

A two-sided stainless steel measuring instrument for precise mixing. Look for double-sided ones with $1/2$- and $3/4$-ounce measures and 1- and 2-ounce cups. A shot glass with measures works, too.

3 MUDDLER

A sturdy tool that's used to crush herbs, sugar cubes and fresh fruit; it's traditionally made of wood.

4 MICROPLANE

A fine-toothed metal grater for shaving citrus zest, ginger and hard spices like cinnamon sticks and nutmeg.

5 JULEP STRAINER

The preferred device for straining cocktails from a mixing glass because it fits securely. Fine holes keep ice out of the drink.

6 CHANNEL KNIFE

A small, spoon-shaped knife with a metal tooth. Creates long, thin spiral-cut twists from citrus-fruit peels.

7 CITRUS JUICER

A metal or ceramic citrus press that allows you to squeeze lemons, limes and oranges *à la minute*.

8 Y PEELER

A wide peeler that's great for making large and small citrus-fruit twists.

9 FINE STRAINER

A fine-mesh strainer held over a glass before the cocktail is poured in (see Fine-Straining Drinks, p. 23). It keeps bits of muddled herbs, fruit and crushed ice out of drinks.

10 WAITER'S CORKSCREW

A pocketknife-like tool with an attached bottle opener. Bartenders prefer it to bulkier, more complicated corkscrews.

11 BOSTON SHAKER

The bartender's choice: consists of a mixing glass, usually a pint glass, with a metal canister that covers the glass to create a seal. Shake drinks with the metal half pointing away from you. Alternatively, replace the mixing glass with a small shaking tin.

12 ICE PICK

A sharp metal tool with a sturdy handle used to break off chunks from a larger block of ice.

13 ATOMIZER

A small spray bottle used to disperse tiny quantities of aromatic liquid evenly over the surface of an empty glass or on top of a cocktail.

14 COBBLER SHAKER

A shaker with a metal cup for mixing drinks with ice, a built-in strainer and a fitted top.

15 BAR SPOON

A long-handled metal spoon that mixes cocktails without creating air bubbles. Some include a relish fork for garnishes.

ESSENTIAL SPIRITS

Trends may be evanescent, but these spirits are still the backbone of a great cocktail list.

VODKA

Produced all over the world, vodka is traditionally distilled from fermented grain or potatoes, but nearly any fruit or vegetable can be used, from grapes to beets. Most **flavored** vodkas are created by adding ingredients to a neutral spirit; the best macerate citrus, berries or herbs in high-proof alcohol.

GIN

Gin is made by distilling a neutral grain spirit with botanicals such as juniper, coriander and citrus peels. The most ubiquitous style is **London dry. Plymouth gin** is less dry and juniper-forward, while **Old Tom** gin is slightly sweeter than London dry. **New Western** gins, such as Hendrick's, incorporate unusual botanicals like rose petals. **Genever,** a predecessor to gin, is a botanically rich, malted grain–based spirit. **Aquavit,** like gin, is made from a neutral alcohol and botanicals such as caraway, citrus peels and star anise.

TEQUILA

Authentic tequila is made from 100 percent blue agave that is harvested by hand, slow-roasted in ovens, fermented, then distilled. **Blanco** (white) tequila is unaged. **Reposado** (rested) tequila, *above*, ages up to one year in barrels. **Añejo** (aged) tequila must be matured between one and three years. **Mezcal** is known for its smoky flavor, which comes from roasting the agave in earthen pits; the finest mezcals are unaged. **Sotol** is a grassy, vegetal spirit made from a desert plant.

RUM

Distilled from sugarcane or its residues, rums are typically produced in tropical regions. **White,** a.k.a. silver or light, rum can be aged, then filtered to remove color. **Amber** (or gold) rum, *above*, is often aged in barrels for a short time; caramel is sometimes added for color. **Dark** rums, made with molasses, include **blackstrap** rum, a rich, thick variety produced from blackstrap molasses; and **Demerara** rum, made on the banks of Guyana's Demerara River, with a burnt-sugar flavor. **Rhum agricole** and **cachaça** are distilled from fresh sugarcane juice.

WHISKEY

Whiskey is distilled from a fermented mash of grains, then typically matured in oak barrels. Scotland and Japan are famous for their **single malts** (produced from 100 percent malted barley from one distillery). **Highland Scotches** are single malts of various styles from Scotland's Highland area. Most **peated** whisky comes from Islay in Scotland. Canada favors **blended** whiskies high in rye. America is known for its **bourbon,** robust **rye** and unaged **white** whiskeys. **Irish** whiskeys tend to be mellow blends.

BRANDY

Brandies are distilled from a fermented mash of fruit. French grape brandies like **Armagnac** and **Cognac** are named for the regions where they are made. **Calvados** is brandy made from apples (and sometimes pears) in the Normandy region of France. **Applejack** is an American apple brandy blended with neutral spirits. Other styles include **pisco,** distilled from aromatic grapes in Peru and Chile; and **eau-de-vie,** a specialty of the European Alps, distilled from a fermented fruit mash and bottled without aging.

APERITIFS (wine-based)

The word *aperitif* is often used to refer to any pre-dinner drink, but aperitifs are also a category of beverage: light, dry and low-proof, with characteristic bitter flavors. A century ago, mixologists began adding wine-based aperitifs to cocktails instead of simply serving them on their own before meals. Wine-based aperitifs include **quinquinas** (or kinas); these contain quinine, a bitter extract from cinnamon-like cinchona bark. Some well-known examples are Lillet, *above,* and Dubonnet.

APERITIFS (spirit-based)

Low-proof, bitter spirit-based aperitifs like **Campari,** *above,* have always been popular in Europe. Now they're beloved in the US thanks to mixologists' embrace of bottles like **Aperol,** the bitter orange Italian aperitif. Other examples of spirit-based aperitifs are **Pimm's No. 1,** a gin-based English aperitif with subtle spice and citrus flavors; and **Cynar,** which is made from 13 herbs and plants, including artichokes.

VERMOUTH

Vermouth is an aromatic fortified wine flavored with botanicals. **Dry** vermouth, *above*, is a staple in martinis. **Sweet** vermouth, which is red, is best known as whiskey's partner in a Manhattan. Italian **bianco** and French **blanc** represent another style that's slightly sweeter than dry vermouth; **rosé** and **rosato** vermouths are pink, with a spicy flavor. **Cocchi Vermouth di Torino** is an Italian red vermouth that's drier and more complex than other red vermouths.

AMARO

Amaro ("bitter" in Italian) is a bittersweet sipping spirit made by infusing or distilling a neutral spirit with herbs, spices, citrus peels or nuts before sweetening and bottling. Traditionally served after dinner to aid digestion, amari like Ramazzotti, Zucca and Nonino, *above*, are popular with American bartenders for the complexity and balance they add to cocktails.

LIQUEURS

Among the oldest spirits, liqueurs are produced from a base alcohol that's distilled or macerated with a variety of ingredients, then sweetened. Sugar makes up to 35 percent of a liqueur's weight by volume, and up to 40 percent for **crème liqueurs** such as crème de menthe. Liqueurs can be herbal **(Chartreuse);** citrus- or fruit-based **(Cointreau);** floral (violet-inflected **parfait amour,** *above*); or nut- or seed-based (**nocino,** made from unripe green walnuts).

BAR LEXICON

ABSINTHE An herbal spirit, formerly banned in the US, flavored with botanicals such as wormwood, green anise and fennel seeds.

ALLSPICE DRAM Also known as pimento dram; a rum-based liqueur infused with Jamaican allspice berries.

APEROL A vibrant orange-red aperitif flavored with bitter orange, rhubarb, gentian and cinchona bark.

APPLEJACK An American apple brandy blended with neutral spirits.

BAROLO CHINATO A Nebbiolo-based fortified wine (produced in Piedmont's Barolo zone)

infused with cinchona bark (*china* in Italian) and various roots, herbs and spices, including rhubarb and cardamom.

BATAVIA-ARRACK VAN OOSTEN A spicy and citrusy rum-like spirit made in Java from sugarcane and fermented red rice.

BÉNÉDICTINE An herbal liqueur with flavors of hyssop, angelica, juniper and myrrh. According to legend, the recipe was developed by a French monk in 1510.

BIGALLET CHINA-CHINA A bitter orange French liqueur made with cinchona, gentian and lots of other spices and herbs. It gets its rich brown color from caramel.

BITTERS Concentrated tinctures of bitter and aromatic herbs, roots and spices that add complexity to drinks. Varieties include orange, chocolate and aromatic bitters, the best known of which is **Angostura. Fee Brothers**

come in 17 flavors and have been made in Rochester, New York, since Prohibition. **Peychaud's** bitters have flavors of anise and cherry.

BONAL GENTIANE-QUINA A slightly bitter French aperitif wine infused with gentian root and cinchona bark, the source of quinine.

BONDED A term used for a single-distillery-produced liquor (such as whiskey or apple brandy) that's distilled during a single season, aged at least four years, bottled at 100 proof and stored in a "bonded" warehouse under US government supervision.

BRANCA MENTA *(above)* A spin-off of the bitter Italian digestif Fernet-Branca (p. 18) with a pronounced peppermint and menthol flavor.

CAMPARI A potent, bright red aperitif with a bitter orange flavor. It's made from a secret blend of fruit, herbs and spices.

CARDAMARO A Moscato-wine-based amaro infused with cardoon, an artichoke-like plant with a nutty flavor; and blessed thistle, a bitter botanical.

CARPANO ANTICA FORMULA *(opposite left)* A rich and complex sweet red vermouth with notes of vanilla. It was invented in Turin, Italy, in 1786.

CHARTREUSE An intense herbal French liqueur made from more than 100 botanicals; **green** Chartreuse is more potent than the honey-sweetened **yellow** one *(right)*.

COCCHI AMERICANO A white-wine-based aperitif infused with cinchona bark, citrus peels and herbs such as gentian. The **rosa** variety is more bitter and aromatic than the **white** *(opposite right)*.

COCCHI VERMOUTH DI TORINO A slightly bitter, Moscato-based red vermouth with hints of citrus, rhubarb and cocoa.

COGNAC (p. 14) is divided into categories based on aging time: **VS** (Very Special) Cognacs are aged at least two years. **VSOP** (Very Superior Old Pale) must be aged at least four years. **XO** (Extra Old) are aged at least ten years.

COINTREAU A French triple sec (p. 19) made with sun-dried sweet and bitter orange peels.

COMBIER PAMPLEMOUSSE ROSE A pale pink French liqueur made by infusing ripe red grapefruit in a neutral alcohol.

CRÈME DE CACAO A cacao-flavored liqueur that's less sweet than chocolate liqueur. It can be **dark** (brown) or **white** (colorless).

CURAÇAO A general term for orange-flavored liqueurs historically produced in the French West Indies. **Blue** curaçao is the same orange-flavored liqueur that has been dyed a vivid blue.

CYNAR A pleasantly bitter aperitif made from 13 herbs and plants, including artichokes.

DRAMBUIE A whisky-based Scottish liqueur flavored with honey, herbs and spices.

FERNET-BRANCA A potent, bitter-flavored Italian digestif that's made from 27 herbs.

GÉNÉPY DES ALPES A pungent herbal liqueur made from génépy, a rare Alpine plant also used in Chartreuse (p. 17).

GUM SYRUP A simple syrup that's been thickened with gum arabic, made from the sap of acacia trees.

HERBSAINT *(above)* An anise-flavored absinthe substitute produced in New Orleans.

LICOR 43 A citrus-and-vanilla-flavored Spanish liqueur made from a combination of 43 aromatic herbs and spices.

LILLET A wine-based aperitif flavored with orange peel and quinine. The **rouge** variety is sweeter than the **blanc.** The **rosé** (a blend of the red and white) has a slightly fruity flavor.

MARASCHINO LIQUEUR A colorless Italian liqueur. The best brands are distilled from sour marasca cherries and their pits, then aged and sweetened with sugar.

ORGEAT A sweet syrup made from almonds or almond extract and rose or orange flower water.

OVERPROOF A term for any spirit (such as bourbon, rum or Cognac) that contains more than 50 percent alcohol (and so is over 100 proof).

PASTIS *(above right)* A licorice-flavored French spirit that turns cloudy

when mixed with water. It's similar to absinthe (p. 16) but sweeter, lower in alcohol and made without wormwood.

PIMM'S NO. 1 A gin-based English aperitif flavored with spices and citrus. It's often served with ginger beer, 7-Up or lemonade.

PORT A fortified wine from the Douro region of Portugal. Styles include fruity, young **ruby** port; richer, nuttier **tawny;** dry or sweet **white** port made from white grapes; and thick-textured, oak-aged **late-bottled vintage (LBV).**

PUNT E MES A spicy, orange-accented Italian sweet vermouth fortified with bitters.

SALERS (*above*) A French gentian root-based aperitif. It has a pronounced bitterness that's balanced by sweetness from white wine and botanicals.

SHERRY A fortified wine from Spain's Jerez region. Varieties include dry styles like **fino** and **manzanilla;** nuttier, richer **amontillado** and **oloroso;** and viscous, sweet **Pedro Ximénez (PX), Moscatel** and **cream** sherry. **East India** sherry falls between an oloroso and a PX in style.

SHOCHU A Japanese low-proof spirit distilled from a variety of ingredients, such as rice, barley, sweet potatoes, buckwheat, carrots or brown sugar.

ST-GERMAIN A French liqueur created by blending macerated elderflower blossoms with eau-de-vie. It has hints of pear, peach and grapefruit zest.

SUZE A bittersweet, aromatic yellow aperitif made from gentian root with hints of vanilla, candied orange and spice.

TREMONTIS MIRTO A bittersweet liqueur from Sardinia that's made from myrtle berries.

TRIPLE SEC An orange-flavored liqueur that is similar to curaçao (p. 17) but not as sweet. **Cointreau,** created in 1875, is the most famous. **Combier,** created in 1834, claims to be the world's first.

VELVET FALERNUM A low-alcohol, sugarcane-based liqueur from Barbados flavored with clove, almond and lime.

VERJUS The tart, pressed, unfermented juice of

unripe grapes. Verjus can be **white** (made from white grapes; *above*) or **red** (made from all red grapes or a mix of red and white).

ZIRBENZ STONE PINE LIQUEUR A slightly sweet liqueur made from the fruit of the arolla stone pine in Austria. It has a reddish hue and a strong pine aroma and flavor.

ZUCCA A bittersweet, slightly smoky aperitif made from rhubarb and flavored with cardamom, citrus and vanilla.

ZWACK An intense, citrus-flavored Hungarian herbal liqueur made from a blend of more than 40 herbs and spices.

MIXOLOGY BASICS

RIMMING A GLASS

MAKING A TWIST

RIMMING A GLASS

Spread salt (preferably kosher), sugar or another powdered ingredient on a small plate.

Moisten half or all of the outer rim of a glass with a citrus-fruit wedge, water or syrup; roll the rim on the plate until it is lightly coated, then tap to release any excess.

MAKING A TWIST

A small strip of citrus zest adds concentrated citrus flavor from the peel's essential oils.

A standard twist

Use a sharp paring knife or peeler to cut a thin, oval disk of the peel, avoiding the pith.

Grasp the twist skin side down and pinch it over the drink. Then discard the twist, set it on the rim or drop it into the drink.

A spiral-cut twist

Working over the drink, use a channel knife (p. 10) to cut a long (about 3 inches), narrow piece of peel with some pith intact.

Wrap the twist around a straw; tighten at both ends to create a curlicue.

FLAMING A TWIST

Flaming an orange or lemon twist caramelizes its essential oils.

Gently grasp a standard citrus twist skin side down about 4 inches over the drink.

Hold a lit match an inch away from the twist– don't let the flame touch the peel–then sharply pinch the twist so the citrus oils fall through the flame and into the drink.

FLAMING
A TWIST

STIRRING
A DRINK
LIKE A PRO

FINE-STRAINING A DRINK

CRACKING ICE

STIRRING DRINKS

To mix drinks like a pro, stir gently and quietly for 20 seconds without rattling the ice.

FINE-STRAINING DRINKS

Removing tiny fruit or herb particles makes your drink look cleaner.

Make your drink in a shaker or mixing glass and set a Hawthorne or julep strainer (p. 10) on top. Hold a fine strainer (p. 11) over the serving glass, then pour the drink through both strainers into the glass.

SMACKING HERBS

Gently clapping fresh herbs between your hands accentuates their aromas and releases essential oils into the drink.

THE RIGHT ICE

Big blocks of ice for punch
Pour water into a large, shallow plastic container and freeze. To unmold, let the container sit briefly at room temperature. Alternatively, buy large blocks from local ice purveyors.

Perfect ice cubes
Use flexible silicone ice molds (available from tovolo.com) to make precisely square cubes or large cubes for rocks glasses. Or make a large block of ice in a loaf pan and use an ice pick to break off chunks.

Crushed ice
Wrap ice cubes in a clean kitchen towel, then pound them with a wooden mallet or rolling pin.

Cracked ice
Put an ice cube in your hand and tap it with the back of a bar spoon until it breaks into pieces.

HOMEMADE
GRENADINE

HOMEMADE MIXERS

SIMPLE SYRUP
Makes about 12 oz.
In a small saucepan, combine 8 oz. water and 1 cup sugar and bring to a boil. Simmer over moderate heat, stirring frequently, until the sugar is dissolved, about 3 minutes. Let cool, then transfer the syrup to a bottle or jar and refrigerate for up to 1 month.

EASIEST SIMPLE SYRUP
Makes about 12 oz.
In a heatproof bottle or jar with a tight-fitting lid, combine 8 oz. hot water with 1 cup superfine sugar and shake until the sugar is dissolved. Let cool, then refrigerate the syrup for up to 1 month.

RICH SIMPLE SYRUP
Makes about 8 oz.
In a small saucepan, combine 4 oz. water and 1 cup Demerara or other raw sugar and bring to a boil. Simmer over moderate heat, stirring, until the sugar is dissolved, about 3 minutes. Let cool, then transfer the syrup to a bottle or jar and refrigerate for up to 1 month.

HOMEMADE GRENADINE
Makes about 12 oz.
In a bottle or jar with a tight-fitting lid, shake 8 oz. unsweetened pomegranate juice with 1 cup sugar until the sugar is dissolved. If desired, add 1/8 teaspoon orange flower water. Refrigerate for up to 2 weeks.

HONEY SYRUP
Makes about 6 oz.
In a microwavable bottle or jar, heat 4 oz. honey in a microwave for about 30 seconds at high power. Add 4 oz. warm water, cover tightly and shake until the honey is dissolved. (Alternatively, in a small saucepan, stir 4 oz. honey and 4 oz. water over moderate heat until the honey is dissolved.) Let cool, then refrigerate for up to 1 month.

THE DOUBTING
DUCK, P. 35

SONOMA
P. 28

LOW-PROOF
+ APERITIF

It's easier than ever for bartenders to create phenomenal low-proof drinks. **A big reason is the explosion of ingredients like vermouths, sherries and European bottled aperitifs in the US. These lighter cocktails don't dull the appetite, so they're perfect for day drinking and before or with dinner.**

GOLDEN SPRITZ

MAKES	**1 drink**
BASE	**Salers**

Salers, a traditional French aperitif made from the bitter root of the gentian plant, has become a pet mixer among US bartenders. At Herbs & Rye in Las Vegas, Emily Yett adds the yellow liqueur to her crisp vermouth spritz.

1¼ oz. Salers
1 oz. Italian bianco vermouth, preferably Contratto
Ice
2 oz. chilled club soda
2 oz. chilled Prosecco
1 lemon twist, for garnish

In a mixing glass, combine the Salers and vermouth. Fill the glass with ice and stir well. Strain into a large chilled flute, stir in the club soda and top with the Prosecco. Pinch the twist over the drink and add to the flute. —*Emily Yett*

●●●●●●●●●

SONOMA

MAKES	**1 drink**
BASE	**White wine**

Devon Tarby of L.A.'s Walker Inn uses an unoaked Chardonnay here because it won't overwhelm the other ingredients in this refreshing cocktail. To make all the subtle flavors pop, she stirs in a couple of drops of a saltwater solution–which can also be added to tart drinks, like a daiquiri.

📷 p. 26

2½ oz. chilled unoaked Chardonnay
½ oz. Calvados
2½ tsp. Honey Syrup (p. 25)
1 tsp. verjus
2 drops of Salt Solution (below)
Ice
1 lemon twist and 1 thyme sprig, for garnish

In a mixing glass, combine the Chardonnay, Calvados, Honey Syrup, verjus and Salt Solution. Fill the glass with ice, stir well and strain into a chilled wineglass. Pinch the lemon twist over the drink and add to the glass. Garnish with the thyme sprig. —*Devon Tarby*

SALT SOLUTION
In a measuring cup, combine 100 ml (about 3½ oz.) water with 5½ tsp. kosher salt and stir until the salt is dissolved. Let stand for 10 minutes. Transfer to a jar and keep at room temperature for up to 1 month. Makes 3½ oz. —*DT*

● STRONG ● SWEET ● TART ● BITTER ● FRUITY ● HERBAL ● SMOKY ● SPICY

GOLDEN
SPRITZ

VALHALLA
RISING

SUNLESS SEA

MAKES **1 drink**

BASE **Pear liqueur and vermouth**

"I love this drink because it gets all of the senses engaged but doesn't dull the palate in the least," says Kyle Linden Webster, co-owner of Expatriate in Portland, Oregon. "You've got the softness of grapefruit liqueur and the tart hit of lime, plus great spice from ancho chile liqueur."

¾ oz. pear liqueur
¾ oz. Carpano Bianco or other Italian bianco vermouth
½ oz. fresh lime juice
¼ oz. grapefruit liqueur, preferably Combier Pamplemousse Rose
¼ oz. Ancho Reyes ancho chile liqueur
Dash of grapefruit bitters
Ice
1 grapefruit twist, for garnish

In a cocktail shaker, combine the pear liqueur, vermouth, lime juice, grapefruit liqueur, chile liqueur and grapefruit bitters. Fill the shaker with ice and shake well. Strain into a chilled coupe. Pinch the grapefruit twist over the drink and add to the glass. —*Kyle Linden Webster*

•••••••
VALHALLA RISING

MAKES **1 drink**

BASE **Aquavit and sherry**

Nico de Soto, co-owner of Mace in New York City, gives this aquavit-sherry cocktail a zingy kick with fresh ginger juice.

1½ oz. Spicy Ginger Syrup (p. 177)
1 oz. Linie aquavit
1 oz. oloroso sherry
¾ oz. fresh lime juice
Ice
4 oz. chilled pale ale
1 piece of candied ginger skewered on a pick, for garnish

In a cocktail shaker, combine the Spicy Ginger Syrup, aquavit, sherry and lime juice. Fill the shaker with ice and shake well. Strain into a chilled, ice-filled highball glass. Stir in the pale ale and garnish with the candied ginger. —*Nico de Soto*

CHATHAM COCKTAIL

MAKES **1 drink**

BASE **Sherry and Cocchi Americano**

As a child, Devon Tarby, co-owner of L.A.'s Walker Inn, often vacationed in Cape Cod with her family. "I imagine this would be the perfect, dry cocktail to enjoy in the summer on the deck overlooking the Atlantic," she says.

¾ oz manzanilla sherry

¾ oz. Cocchi Americano (fortified, slightly bitter aperitif wine)

½ oz. fresh lemon juice

¼ oz. Grand Marnier

¼ oz. Simple Syrup (p. 25)

Ice

2 oz. chilled French sparkling wine

1 grapefruit twist

In a cocktail shaker, combine the sherry, Cocchi Americano, lemon juice, Grand Marnier and Simple Syrup. Fill the shaker with ice and shake well. Strain into a chilled flute. Top with the sparkling wine, then pinch the grapefruit twist over the drink and discard. —*Devon Tarby*

NORMANDIE CLUB SPRITZ

MAKES **1 drink**

BASE **Vermouth**

Devon Tarby features this lovely, light spritz at The Normandie Club in L.A. "It's like the best grapefruit soda you can imagine," she says, "and tame enough that you can chug a few."

1 oz. dry vermouth, preferably Dolin

1 oz. St-Germain elderflower liqueur

1 oz. fresh grapefruit juice

½ oz. fresh lemon juice

¼ oz. grapefruit liqueur

¼ oz. blanco tequila

¼ oz. pisco, preferably Campo de Encanto

Ice

2½ oz. chilled club soda

1 grapefruit wheel half, for garnish

In a cocktail shaker, combine the vermouth, St-Germain, grapefruit juice, lemon juice, grapefruit liqueur, tequila and pisco. Fill the shaker with ice and shake for 5 seconds. Strain into a chilled, ice-filled collins glass. Stir in the club soda and garnish with the grapefruit wheel half. —*Devon Tarby*

● STRONG ● SWEET ● TART ● BITTER ● FRUITY ● HERBAL ● SMOKY ● SPICY

NORMANDIE
CLUB SPRITZ

AIR BAG

MAKES **1 drink**

BASE **Cocchi Americano**

Mirto, a bitter, cassis-like liqueur that's made from myrtle berries, is served as a complimentary digestif at almost every restaurant in Sardinia. At Expatriate in Portland, Oregon, Kyle Linden Webster used the liqueur in a low-proof aperitif for a friend facing a long drive home.

1½ oz. Cocchi Americano (fortified, slightly bitter aperitif wine)
¾ oz. Tremontis mirto liqueur
¾ oz. dry vermouth, preferably Dolin
¾ oz. fresh lime juice
Ice
1 lime twist, for garnish

In a cocktail shaker, combine the Cocchi Americano, mirto, vermouth and lime juice. Fill the shaker with ice and shake well. Strain into a chilled, ice-filled rocks glass. Pinch the lime twist over the drink and add to the glass. —*Kyle Linden Webster*

LILY OF THE VALLEY

MAKES **1 drink**

BASE **Gin**

"This cocktail screams Southern California to me." says L.A. mixology consultant Karen Grill. "It's tart and citrusy, with cooling flavors from aloe liqueur, making this a perfect aperitif." If aloe liqueur is unavailable, swap in aloe juice (available at health food stores).

1½ oz. London dry gin
¾ oz. fresh lime juice
½ oz. aloe vera liqueur or juice
¼ oz. Simple Syrup (p. 25)
¼ oz. agave syrup
Ice
2 oz. chilled club soda
1½ oz. chilled dry rosé
1 lime twist and edible flowers (optional), for garnish

In a cocktail shaker, combine the gin, lime juice, aloe liqueur, Simple Syrup and agave syrup. Fill the shaker with ice and shake for 5 seconds. Strain into a chilled, ice-filled collins glass. Stir in the club soda, then float the rosé on top, slowly pouring it over the back of a bar spoon near the drink's surface. Pinch the lime twist over the drink and add to the glass; garnish with edible flowers. —*Karen Grill*

CHRISTMAS TREE GIMLET

MAKES **1 drink**

BASE **Shochu**

Bartender Nico de Soto created this yuletide cocktail for Miracle on Ninth Street, his kitschy, holiday-themed pop-up in New York City. De Soto sous vides Christmas tree pine needles to make his own cordial. A good alternative is bottled pinecone bud syrup, available from amazon.com.

2 oz. sweet potato or carrot shochu, such as Kaikouzu

1 oz. Mugolio pinecone bud syrup

Ice

1 grapefruit twist, for garnish

In a mixing glass, combine the shochu and pinecone bud syrup. Fill the glass with ice and stir well. Strain into a chilled coupe. Pinch the grapefruit twist over the drink and add to the glass. —*Nico de Soto*

THE DOUBTING DUCK

MAKES **1 drink**

BASE **Sherry**

Washington, DC, bartender Derek Brown calls The Doubting Duck his ideal aperitif because while it's low-proof, it's also amazingly complex. He loves the manzanilla sherry's savory edge, which makes the drink incredibly food-friendly.

📷 p. 26

1½ oz. manzanilla sherry

1 oz. dry vermouth

½ oz. yellow Chartreuse (honeyed herbal liqueur)

Dash of celery bitters

Dash of orange bitters

Ice

1 lemon twist skewered on a pick with 1 olive, for garnish

In a mixing glass, combine the sherry, vermouth, Chartreuse and both bitters. Fill the glass with ice and stir well. Strain into a chilled coupe and garnish with the skewered lemon twist and olive. —*Derek Brown*

● STRONG ● SWEET ● TART ● BITTER ● FRUITY ● HERBAL ● SMOKY ● SPICY

TANGLED UP

MAKES **1 drink**

BASE **Sherry**

"In southern Spain, they love rebujitos," says Washington, DC, bartender Derek Brown about the sherry–lemon soda spritzer. He gives his version a pleasantly bitter boost with Suze, a French aperitif. "It's refreshing," he says, "but you get a little more than just sweet and easy."

2 oz. oloroso or cream sherry
¼ oz. Suze
Ice
4 oz. bitter lemon soda or San Pellegrino Limonata
1 spiral-cut lemon twist (p. 20), for garnish

In a chilled highball glass, combine the sherry and Suze. Fill the glass with ice and stir well. Stir in the lemon soda and garnish with the lemon twist. —*Derek Brown*

DAISY CHAIN

MAKES **1 drink**

BASE **Sherry**

To maintain the balance of this apple-inflected aperitif, be sure to use dry types of Riesling and cider.

1½ oz. manzanilla sherry
½ oz. St-Germain elderflower liqueur
½ oz. chilled dry Riesling
¼ oz. Suze (bittersweet gentian aperitif)
¼ oz. fresh lemon juice
2 drops of Salt Solution (p. 28)
Ice
3 oz. chilled dry French apple cider, such as Le Père Jules
1 mint sprig, for garnish

In a chilled wineglass, combine the sherry, St-Germain, Riesling, Suze, lemon juice and Salt Solution. Fill the glass with ice and stir well. Stir in the cider and garnish with the mint sprig. —*Devon Tarby*

● STRONG ● SWEET ● TART ● BITTER ● FRUITY ● HERBAL ● SMOKY ● SPICY

FOUR ON
THE FLOOR
P. 46

BRUNCH

As chefs create more
ambitious brunch dishes,
bartenders are stepping
up their drinks game, too.
These midday concoctions
are just as sophisticated
as the cocktails served at
night. Light and often spritzy
and fruity, they're fantastic
with eggs and the rich food
served at brunch.

BRUNCH ON THE DANUBE

MAKES **1 drink**

BASE **Zwack**

Bryan Dayton, beverage director and co-owner of Oak at Fourteenth in Boulder, Colorado, adds complex herbal flavors to this fizzy aperitif with Zwack, an amaro-like Hungarian liqueur. In the US, many bartenders turn to it as an alternative to Jägermeister.

¾ oz. Zwack

½ oz. tawny port

¼ oz. walnut liqueur, such as Nocino della Cristina

¼ oz. Simple Syrup (p. 25)
  Ice

3 oz. chilled ginger beer

1 orange twist, for garnish

In a mixing glass, combine the Zwack, port, walnut liqueur and Simple Syrup. Fill the glass with ice and stir well. Strain into a chilled, ice-filled collins glass, then stir in the ginger beer. Pinch the orange twist over the drink and add to the glass. —*Bryan Dayton*

●●●●●●●●●

CDT SUNSET

MAKES **1 drink**

BASE **Pimm's and Campari**

Colorado bartender Bryan Dayton makes a juiced-up Aperol spritz using Campari, Aperol's more bracing cousin. The color of the drink reminds Dayton of beautiful sunsets he's seen from the Continental Divide Trail.

3 mint leaves

¼ oz. Simple Syrup (p. 25)

½ oz. Pimm's No. 1 (gin-based aperitif)

½ oz. Campari

½ oz. peach liqueur, such as Mathilde

½ oz. fresh orange juice

¼ oz. fresh lime juice
  Ice

1½ oz. chilled cava

In a cocktail shaker, muddle 2 of the mint leaves with the Simple Syrup. Add the Pimm's, Campari, peach liqueur, orange juice and lime juice. Fill the shaker with ice and shake well. Fine-strain (p. 23) into a chilled flute and top with the cava. Smack (p. 23) the remaining mint leaf over the drink and add to the glass. —*Bryan Dayton*

●STRONG ●SWEET ●TART ●BITTER ●FRUITY ●HERBAL ●SMOKY ●SPICY

BRUNCH
ON THE DANUBE

ESPECIA DE PINYA

GOING DUTCH

MAKES **1 drink**

BASE **Genever**

"This malty julep with a touch of bubbles has such incredible texture," says Karen Grill, bartender at Melrose Umbrella Co. in L.A. The Dutch-style gin called genever gives the drink a maltiness reminiscent of whisky.

1 mint leaf, plus 1 mint sprig for garnish
¾ oz. lemon syrup (available from amazon.com)
2 oz. genever
Crushed ice (p. 23)
3 oz. chilled sparkling wine
Pinch of salt
1 lemon twist rolled and skewered on a pick, for garnish

In a chilled highball glass, muddle the mint leaf with the lemon syrup. Stir in the genever and top with crushed ice. Add the sparkling wine and salt. Garnish with the mint sprig and the skewered lemon twist. —*Karen Grill*

ESPECIA DE PINYA

MAKES **1 drink**

BASE **Tequila**

As a Bloody Mary nonfan, New York City bartender Pamela Wiznitzer set out to remake the tomato-based brunch staple. "I LOVE this recipe," she gushes. "It has intense spices, fruitiness and loads of nutrients, too! It's like going through detox and retox simultaneously."

1½ oz. yellow tomato puree
1 oz. fresh pineapple juice
¾ oz. fresh lemon juice
¾ oz. fresh orange juice
1 tsp. sherry vinegar
1 tsp. extra-virgin olive oil
Pinch of ground sea salt
Pinch of ground pink peppercorns
½ tsp. diced habanero chiles, preferably grilled
2 oz. reposado tequila
Ice
1 pineapple wedge skewered on a pick with 1 yellow cherry tomato, for garnish

In a cocktail shaker, combine all of the ingredients except the ice and garnish. Shake well. Fill the shaker with ice and shake again. Fine-strain (p. 23) into a chilled, ice-filled highball glass. Garnish with the skewered pineapple and cherry tomato.
—*Pamela Wiznitzer*

● STRONG ● SWEET ● TART ● BITTER ● FRUITY ● HERBAL ● SMOKY ● SPICY

FRUIT COBBLER

MAKES **1 drink**

BASE **Apricot liqueur**

Emily Yett, bartender at Herbs & Rye in Las Vegas, mixes tonic syrup into her citrusy cobbler. It's a terrific way to add the concentrated bitterness of tonic water without the soda-pop sweetness of most commercial brands. Look for small-batch bottles like Tomr's (tomrstonic.com).

1 slice each of lemon, lime and orange

1½ oz. Rothman & Winter Orchard Apricot liqueur

½ oz. Luxardo maraschino liqueur

¼ oz. homemade or store-bought tonic syrup (the syrupy base for tonic water)

Crushed ice (p. 23)

1 mint sprig, for garnish

In a chilled julep cup or rocks glass, muddle the lemon, lime and orange slices. Add the apricot liqueur, maraschino liqueur and tonic syrup. Fill the cup with crushed ice. Spin a swizzle stick or bar spoon between your hands to mix the drink. Top with more crushed ice and garnish with the mint sprig. —*Emily Yett*

TRICK PONY

MAKES **1 drink**

BASE **Sherry**

"The name of this cocktail pokes fun at my love of apple brandy–and sherry, for that matter," says Devon Tarby, co-owner of L.A.'s Normandie Club. She boosts the fresh apple flavor of the drink with cider, giving the ingredients a brief shake with ice to chill them.

1½ oz. fino sherry

1 oz. fresh apple cider

½ oz. applejack, such as Laird's

½ oz. fresh lemon juice

¼ oz. Honey Syrup (p. 25)

Ice

3 oz. chilled club soda

3 thin apple slices, for garnish

In a cocktail shaker, combine the sherry, apple cider, applejack, lemon juice and Honey Syrup. Fill the shaker with ice and shake for 5 seconds. Strain into a chilled, ice-filled collins glass. Stir in the club soda and garnish with the 3 apple slices arranged in a fan. —*Devon Tarby*

CHANDELIER FLIP

MAKES **1 drink**

BASE **Port**

A flip is a cocktail shaken with a whole egg, resulting in a soft, lush texture. The drink has historically been called "a yard of flannel" for that very reason. Brooklyn mixologist Maxwell Britten gives his flip extra richness with a topping of Angostura whipped cream.

3 oz. heavy cream
2 dashes of Angostura bitters
1 large egg
1¼ oz. port
¾ oz. XO Cognac
¼ oz. Rich Simple Syrup (p. 25)
Ice

1. Remove the spring from a Hawthorne strainer and place in a chilled cocktail shaker. Add the cream and bitters and shake until the cream forms soft peaks. Transfer the whipped cream to a small bowl and wipe out the shaker.

2. In the shaker, combine the egg, port, Cognac and Rich Simple Syrup and shake vigorously. Fill the shaker with ice and shake again. Strain into a chilled wineglass. Top with the Angostura whipped cream. —*Maxwell Britten*

● STRONG ● SWEET ● TART ● BITTER ● FRUITY ● HERBAL ● SMOKY ● SPICY

ROSIE'S RETURN

MAKES **1 drink**

BASE **Gin**

Bryan Dayton likes to serve this pretty pink aperitif before a brunch or dinner celebration at Acorn, his bar and grill in Denver. Just one drop of rose water adds a distinct floral flavor.

3 **raspberries**
¾ **oz. London dry gin**
¾ **oz. Simple Syrup (p. 25)**
½ **oz. fresh lemon juice**
2 **drops of orange bitters**
1 **drop of rose water**
Ice
1½ **oz. chilled sparkling rosé**

In a cocktail shaker, muddle 2 of the raspberries. Add the gin, Simple Syrup, lemon juice, orange bitters and rose water. Fill the shaker with ice and shake well. Strain into a chilled flute. Top with the sparkling rosé and garnish with the remaining raspberry. —*Bryan Dayton*

FOUR ON THE FLOOR

MAKES **1 drink**

BASE **Sherry**

"This drink is rich and nutty, with ripe fruits that toe the line of winter and spring," says L.A. bartender Karen Grill. "It reminds me of January in Los Angeles."

📷 **p. 38**

2 **strawberries, 2 raspberries and 2 blackberries**
2 **lemon twists**
½ **oz. Cinnamon Syrup (p. 157)**
1 **oz. oloroso sherry, preferably Lustau**
1 **oz. East India sherry**
Crushed ice (p. 23)
1 **mint sprig, for garnish**

In a chilled julep cup or rocks glass, muddle 1 of each of the berries with 1 lemon twist and the Cinnamon Syrup. Add the sherries, then fill the cup with crushed ice. Spin a swizzle stick or bar spoon between your hands to mix the drink. Add more crushed ice and garnish with the remaining berries and lemon twist and the mint sprig. —*Karen Grill*

● STRONG ● SWEET ● TART ● BITTER ● FRUITY ● HERBAL ● SMOKY ● SPICY

ROSIE'S RETURN

HAGAR THE
GENTLE

HAGAR THE GENTLE

MAKES **1 drink**

BASE **Vermouth**

"I want this drink from about noon till 6 p.m.– bartenders can turn brunch into an all-after-noon affair at the slightest provocation," says Joaquín Simó of Pouring Ribbons in New York City. "I'd happily have this food-friendly cocktail alongside some savory scones, soft scrambled eggs and piles of shaved jamón."

1 rosemary sprig
½ oz. Simple Syrup (p. 25)
2 oz. dry vermouth, preferably Dolin
½ oz. Linie aquavit
 Dash of absinthe
 Ice
4 oz. chilled club soda
1 orange wheel half skewered on a rosemary sprig, for garnish

In a cocktail shaker, muddle the rosemary sprig with the Simple Syrup. Add the vermouth, aquavit and absinthe; fill with ice and shake well. Fine-strain (p. 23) into a chilled, ice-filled highball glass and stir in the club soda. Garnish with the skewered orange wheel. —*Joaquín Simó*

COLD IN THE SHADOWS

MAKES **1 drink**

BASE **Campari**

Pamela Wiznitzer featured this refreshing, low-proof cocktail when she opened Seamstress in New York City. It's fruity and tart, with a bitter edge, so it's best before a meal to spark your appetite, she says.

1 oz. Campari
1 oz. fresh lime juice
½ oz. raspberry liqueur
½ oz. Honey Syrup (p. 25)
 Ice cubes, plus crushed ice (p. 23) for serving
1½ oz. chilled IPA-style beer
1 orange wedge and 1 lime wedge, for garnish

In a cocktail shaker, combine the Campari, lime juice, raspberry liqueur and Honey Syrup. Fill the shaker with ice cubes and shake for 5 seconds. Add the beer to the shaker and strain into a chilled, crushed ice–filled highball glass. Garnish with the orange and lime wedges. —*Pamela Wiznitzer*

● STRONG ● SWEET ● TART ● BITTER ● FRUITY ● HERBAL ● SMOKY ● SPICY

GRANNY'S
BRANDY, P. 54

BEET IT
P. 52

JUICE-SPIKED

SILLY RABBIT
P. 55

Mixologists are adding all kinds of fresh, cold-pressed juices to cocktails. Fueling this trend is the ubiquity of juice bars and high-powered juicers and the interest in alternative sweeteners.

BEET IT

MAKES **1 drink**	
BASE **Tequila**	

"I've always felt tequila had a natural affinity for super-earthy ingredients," says San Diego bartender Lindsay Nader, who makes this refreshing cocktail with beets. "Try not to spill, because the stain can be more perilous than red wine!" she warns.

📷 p. 50

2 oz. blanco tequila
1 oz. fresh beet juice
¾ oz. Simple Syrup (p. 25)
½ oz. fresh cucumber juice
½ oz. fresh lime juice
  Ice
1 cucumber ribbon skewered on a pick, for garnish

In a cocktail shaker, combine the tequila, beet juice, Simple Syrup, cucumber juice and lime juice; fill with ice and shake well. Strain into a chilled, ice-filled rocks glass and garnish with the cucumber ribbon. —*Lindsay Nader*

GREEN GODDESS SANGRITA

MAKES **6 drinks**	
BASE **Tequila**	

Joaquín Simó, co-owner of Pouring Ribbons in New York City, created this spicy-sweet take on sangrita, the typically tomato-based chaser for tequila. "The combination of tequila and sangrita is designed to be sipped, not shot," Simó says. "It can be consumed pretty much any time you're relaxing with friends."

4 oz. fresh cucumber juice
4 oz. fresh lime juice
3 oz. fresh jicama juice
3 oz. fresh ginger juice (from a 4-inch piece)
3 oz. fresh green tomatillo juice
  Juice of ⅔ cup well-packed cilantro leaves (see Note)
3 oz. fresh Granny Smith apple juice
  Juice of ¼ serrano chile
2 oz. honey, preferably wildflower
  Pinch of salt and freshly ground white pepper to taste
6 shots of blanco tequila, for serving

In a pitcher, combine the juices, honey, salt and pepper; stir well. Refrigerate until well chilled, about 2 hours. Serve in chilled fizz glasses with the tequila shots alongside. —*Joaquín Simó*

Note To juice cilantro, run it in the juicer with a more fibrous ingredient like apple.

● STRONG ● SWEET ◐ TART ◓ BITTER ● FRUITY ● HERBAL ● SMOKY ● SPICY

GREEN GODDESS
SANGRITA

THE OAXACA CROSS

MAKES **1 drink**

BASE **Mezcal**

Chris Lane, bar manager at Ramen Shop in Oakland, California, calls this drink a successful mash-up of two favorite cocktails: the tequila-based El Diablo and the El Morocco, a brandy sour with pineapple, grenadine and port. Instead of tequila, Lane mixes in smoky mezcal.

1½ oz. mezcal
¾ oz. fresh pineapple juice
½ oz. ruby port
½ oz. Luxardo maraschino liqueur
½ oz. fresh lemon juice
¼ oz. Spicy Ginger Syrup (p. 177)
   Ice
1 orange twist, for garnish

In a cocktail shaker, combine the mezcal, pineapple juice, port, maraschino liqueur, lemon juice and Spicy Ginger Syrup. Fill the shaker with ice and shake well. Strain into a chilled, ice-filled collins glass. Pinch the orange twist over the drink and add to the glass. —*Chris Lane*

GRANNY'S BRANDY

MAKES **1 drink**

BASE **Pisco**

San Diego bartender Lindsay Nader adds pisco, the South American grape brandy, to this tart, refreshing and slightly herbal juice. Omit the pisco for a mocktail of surprising flavor and complexity.

📷 p. 50

2 oz. pisco, preferably Campo de Encanto Moscatel
2 oz. fresh Granny Smith apple juice
½ oz. fresh celery juice
½ oz. Honey Syrup (p. 25)
¼ oz. fresh fennel juice
   Ice
2 oz. chilled club soda
1 celery stalk and 1 fennel slice, for garnish

In a cocktail shaker, combine the pisco, apple juice, celery juice, Honey Syrup and fennel juice. Fill the shaker with ice and shake well. Strain into a chilled, ice-filled collins glass and stir in the club soda. Garnish with the celery stalk and fennel slice. —*Lindsay Nader*

SILLY RABBIT

MAKES **1 drink**

BASE **Pear brandy**

For this herbal, spiced juice cocktail, San Diego bartender Lindsay Nader collaborated with Dave Fernie, then manager of the Parisian-style club Pour Vous in L.A. Fernie named the drink Lapin Fou, which means "silly rabbit" in French.

📷 p. 51

1½ oz. pear brandy, preferably Clear Creek
¾ oz. fresh carrot juice
¾ oz. fresh lemon juice
¼ oz. yellow Chartreuse (honeyed herbal liqueur)
¼ oz. Spicy Ginger Syrup (p. 177)
¼ oz. Rich Simple Syrup (p. 25)
   Ice
1 pear fan, for garnish

In a cocktail shaker, combine the pear brandy, carrot juice, lemon juice, Chartreuse, Spicy Ginger Syrup and Rich Simple Syrup. Fill the shaker with ice and shake well. Strain into a large chilled coupe and garnish with the pear fan. —*Lindsay Nader*

●●●●●●●●

VIOLENT FEMME PUNCH

MAKES **1 drink**

BASE **Tequila and sherry**

Sara Justice, general manager of The Franklin Bar in Philadelphia, gives beet juice a tropical makeover with her Violent Femme Punch. "All of the juices make it nice and light and feminine. Then it's spiked with tequila and sherry, so there's more than meets the eye," she says.

1 oz. blanco tequila
1 oz. fino sherry
¾ oz. Spicy Ginger Syrup (p. 177)
¾ oz. fresh pineapple juice
½ oz. fresh lemon juice
¼ oz. Velvet Falernum (clove-spiced liqueur)
¼ oz. fresh beet juice
10 cilantro leaves
   Ice

In a cocktail shaker, combine all of the ingredients except the ice. Fill the shaker with ice and shake well. Strain into a chilled, ice-filled rocks glass. —*Sara Justice*

● STRONG ● SWEET ● TART ● BITTER ● FRUITY ● HERBAL ● SMOKY ● SPICY

ROCK 'N' ROLLA

ROCK 'N' ROLLA

MAKES **1 drink**

BASE **Bourbon**

"I love this drink because it is so immensely accessible and easy to make," says Bay Area bartender Chris Lane. "Really it's just a bourbon sour with a little flourish of spice and apple." Lane's inspiration for the drink: a local biodynamic apple cider.

1½ oz. overproof bourbon, such as Booker's
1 oz. apple juice, preferably organic
¾ oz. fresh lemon juice
½ oz. pure maple syrup
¼ oz. St. Elizabeth allspice liqueur
2 dashes of Angostura bitters
Ice, plus 1 large cube for serving
Pinch of freshly grated nutmeg, for garnish

In a cocktail shaker, combine the bourbon, apple juice, lemon juice, maple syrup, allspice liqueur and bitters. Fill the shaker with ice and shake well. Strain into a chilled double rocks glass over the large cube and garnish with the nutmeg. —*Chris Lane*

RIDGECREST

MAKES **4 drinks**

BASE **Hard cider**

Chad Arnholt and Claire Sprouse, founders of the cocktail consultancy Tin Roof Drink Community, came up with this drink for a special dinner highlighting wild ingredients at the eco-minded Perennial restaurant in San Francisco.

2 oz. strained fresh grapefruit juice
¼ cup superfine sugar
1 Tbsp. pear brandy
8 oz. chilled fresh fennel juice
Ice
8 oz. chilled sparkling hard cider
Fennel fronds, for garnish

1. In a bowl, whisk the grapefruit juice with the sugar and brandy until the sugar is dissolved. Chill the grapefruit cordial for 15 minutes or up to 1 week.

2. In a large liquid measuring cup, stir the fennel juice with 2 oz. of the grapefruit cordial. Pour into 4 ice-filled collins glasses and top with the cider. Garnish the drinks with fennel fronds. —*Chad Arnholt and Claire Sprouse*

COCO COOLER

MAKES **1 drink**

BASE **Vodka**

"This cocktail is a riff on one of my favorite cold-pressed juices: a light-pink, super-hydrating concoction called Aloe Vera Wang," says San Diego bartender Lindsay Nader.

2 oz. fresh watermelon juice
2 oz. coconut water
1½ oz. vodka
¾ oz. Zucca (rhubarb-flavored amaro)
½ oz. fresh lime juice
½ oz. Simple Syrup (p. 25)
  Ice
2 oz. chilled club soda
1 watermelon spear, for garnish

In a cocktail shaker, combine the watermelon juice, coconut water, vodka, Zucca, lime juice and Simple Syrup. Fill the shaker with ice and shake well. Strain into a chilled, ice-filled collins glass. Stir in the club soda and garnish with the watermelon spear. —*Lindsay Nader*

JACK + JUICE

MAKES **1 drink**

BASE **Whiskey**

Lindsay Nader, a founder of Juice Saves juice bar in San Diego, created this drink with Eric Tecosky of Tennessee whiskey distillery Jack Daniel's. They revamp a basic sour by adding sweet pear juice and a good dose of zingy ginger juice.

4 oz. fresh pineapple juice
1½ oz. Tennessee whiskey, preferably Jack Daniel's
1 oz. fresh pear juice
½ oz. fresh lemon juice
½ oz. fresh ginger juice (from a 1½-inch piece of ginger)
¾ tsp. honey
  Ice
3 small pineapple leaves (optional) and 1 maraschino cherry skewered on a pick, for garnish

In a cocktail shaker, combine the pineapple juice, whiskey, pear juice, lemon juice, ginger juice and honey. Fill the shaker with ice and shake well. Strain into a chilled, ice-filled rocks glass and garnish with the pineapple leaves and skewered cherry. —*Lindsay Nader*

● STRONG   ● SWEET   ● TART   ● BITTER   ● FRUITY   ● HERBAL   ● SMOKY   ● SPICY

COCO
COOLER

HIGH-
OCTANE
P. 73

COFFEE+TEA DRINKS

Mixologists are precisely the obsessive types who love to geek out over coffee and tea. Some even started their careers as baristas, before they were legally old enough to mix drinks. So the boom in innovative coffee and tea cocktails is no surprise. Also fueling the trend: the increased availability of cold-brew coffee and high-quality coffee liqueurs and teas, plus the current passion for bitter and intense flavors.

SUBURBAN ANXIETY

MAKES **1 drink**

BASE **Vodka**

Charmed by the idea of a lavender lemonade, Lindsay Ferdinand of Common Quarter in Atlanta created this drink for a bridal shower. "It's bright, bubbly and deliciously different with the hint of lavender–a perfect girls'-day-out drink, but secretly men love it too," she says.

1 oz. vodka
1 oz. Lavender Syrup (below)
½ oz. fresh lemon juice
Ice
2 oz. dry sparkling rosé
1 lavender sprig, for garnish

In a cocktail shaker, combine the vodka, Lavender Syrup and lemon juice. Fill the shaker with ice and shake well. Strain into a chilled coupe, top with the sparkling rosé and garnish with the lavender sprig. —*Lindsay Ferdinand*

LAVENDER SYRUP

In a small saucepan, bring 4 oz. water to a boil and stir in ½ cup sugar. Simmer until dissolved, about 2 minutes. Add 1 Tbsp. dried lavender or 1 lavender tea bag and remove from the heat. Steep the lavender in the hot syrup for 10 minutes. Strain the syrup into a heatproof jar, let cool and refrigerate for up to 2 weeks. Makes about 6 oz. —*LF*

● STRONG ● SWEET ● TART ● BITTER ● FRUITY ● HERBAL ● SMOKY ● SPICY

BOURBON CHAI
MILK PUNCH

BOURBON CHAI MILK PUNCH

MAKES **1 drink**

BASE **Bourbon**

Kenta Goto, owner of New York City's Bar Goto, infuses bourbon with chai tea, then shakes the drink with cream and maple syrup. The result is like a boozy chai latte.

2 oz. Chai Bourbon (below)

¾ oz. heavy cream

½ oz. pure maple syrup

¼ oz. Simple Syrup (p. 25)

Ice

In a cocktail shaker, combine the Chai Bourbon, cream, maple syrup and Simple Syrup; shake vigorously. Fill the shaker with ice and shake again. Strain into a chilled coupe. —*Kenta Goto*

CHAI BOURBON

In a jar, steep 1 Tbsp. loose chai tea in 8 oz. bourbon for 1 hour. Strain and keep at room temperature for up to 1 month. Makes 8 oz. —*KG*

RHINESTONE EYES

MAKES **1 drink**

BASE **Cognac**

Sara Justice, general manager of The Franklin Bar in Philadelphia, infuses Cognac with genmaicha, a Japanese green tea mixed with roasted brown rice (available at Asian markets). It adds a nutty, toasty flavor to this frothy cocktail.

1 tsp. loose genmaicha tea

2 oz. VS Cognac

¾ oz. Persimmon Syrup (below)

¾ oz. fresh lemon juice

6 drops of absinthe

1 large egg white

Ice

In a liquid measuring cup, steep the genmaicha in the Cognac for 10 minutes. Strain into a cocktail shaker. Add the Persimmon Syrup, lemon juice, absinthe and egg white and shake vigorously. Fill the shaker with ice and shake again. Strain into a large chilled coupe. —*Sara Justice*

PERSIMMON SYRUP

In a small bowl, combine ½ cup diced peeled Fuyu persimmons with 1 cup sugar. Cover and let macerate overnight. Add 4 oz. water and stir to dissolve the sugar. Strain into a jar and refrigerate for up to 2 weeks. Makes 6 oz. —*SJ*

● STRONG ● SWEET ● TART ● BITTER ● FRUITY ● HERBAL ● SMOKY ● SPICY

MATCHA MILK PUNCH

MAKES **1 drink**

BASE **Vodka**

Kenta Goto, owner of Bar Goto in New York City, uses two types of green tea in this creamy, milkshake-like cocktail: herbaceous sencha and tannic matcha green tea powder.

2 oz. **Sencha Vodka (below)**
½ oz. **half-and-half**
⅜ oz. **cane syrup mixed with ⅜ oz. water**
⅛ tsp. **matcha green tea powder**
   Ice

In a cocktail shaker, combine the Sencha Vodka, half-and-half, cane syrup and matcha; shake vigorously. Fill with ice, shake again and strain into a chilled tea cup. —*Kenta Goto*

SENCHA VODKA
In a liquid measuring cup, steep 1 Tbsp. loose sencha tea in 8 oz. vodka for 5 minutes. Strain the vodka into a jar and keep at room temperature for up to 1 month. Makes 8 oz. —*KG*

KENTA-MENTA COOLER

MAKES **4 drinks**

BASE **Bourbon**

This bourbon cocktail is a good gateway to Branca Menta, the intensely minty-mentholy digestif that people either love or hate. New York City bartender Kenta Goto adds a little bit of the liqueur to iced mint tea.

1 Tbsp. **loose peppermint tea or 1 peppermint tea bag**
8 oz. **boiling water**
4 oz. **bourbon, preferably Elijah Craig 12-year**
4 oz. **Simple Syrup (p. 25)**
3 oz. **Southern Comfort, preferably 100 proof**
2 oz. **fresh lime juice**
1 oz. **Branca Menta**
   Ice

In a heatproof bowl, steep the tea in the boiling water for 4 minutes. Strain the tea and let cool, then freeze until chilled, 30 minutes. In a cocktail shaker, combine half each of the bourbon, Simple Syrup, Southern Comfort, lime juice and Branca Menta. Fill with ice and shake well. Strain into 2 chilled, ice-filled highball glasses. Stir 2 oz. of the iced tea into each drink. Repeat and serve. —*Kenta Goto*

● STRONG ● SWEET ● TART ● BITTER ● FRUITY ● HERBAL ● SMOKY ● SPICY

MATCHA
MILK PUNCH

PRISMATIC
BLADE

MORNING GLORY

MAKES **1 drink**

BASE **Vodka**

"This recipe is a better variation on the espresso martini, which can be sickly sweet and unbalanced," says Pamela Wiznitzer of Seamstress in New York City. The almond milk makes the drink creamy but not too rich.

2 oz. vodka
1½ oz. Cold-Brew Coffee Concentrate (p. 73)
1 oz. unsweetened almond milk
¾ oz. Rich Simple Syrup (p. 25)
½ oz. vanilla liqueur or syrup
Ice
Pinch of cinnamon, for garnish

In a cocktail shaker, combine the vodka, coffee concentrate, almond milk, Rich Simple Syrup and vanilla liqueur. Fill the shaker with ice and shake well. Strain into a chilled, ice-filled highball glass and garnish with a pinch of cinnamon. —*Pamela Wiznitzer*

PRISMATIC BLADE

MAKES **1 drink**

BASE **Amaro**

For a pop-up event in San Francisco, New Orleans bartender Nick Detrich worked with local cult roasters Sightglass and Spitfire Coffee. Among the exceptional cocktails: this tequila-spiked take on Irish coffee. Detrich tops the drink with a triple sec whipped cream made in a shaker–the removable spring from a Hawthorne strainer whisks the cream into soft peaks.

1 oz. Ramazzotti amaro
¾ oz. añejo tequila
¾ oz. heavy cream
½ oz. triple sec
4 oz. freshly brewed hot coffee, preferably pour-over

1. Fill a large saucepan with water and bring just to a boil; remove from the heat. In a small saucepan, combine the amaro and tequila. Place the small saucepan in the hot water, stirring occasionally, until heated through.

2. Meanwhile, remove the spring from a Hawthorne strainer and place it in a chilled cocktail shaker. Add the cream and triple sec and shake until the cream is softly whipped.

3. Add the coffee to the amaro mixture and stir well. Pour into a warmed mug and top with the triple sec whipped cream. —*Nick Detrich*

● STRONG ● SWEET ● TART ● BITTER ● FRUITY ● HERBAL ● SMOKY ● SPICY

TWO MIRRORS

MAKES **1 drink**	
BASE **Herbsaint**	

"Two Mirrors has a special place in my heart," says New Orleans bartender Nick Detrich. "It's a frappé-style drink with a good dash of anise and floral notes like the absinthe frappés of Mardi Gras." To garnish with rose water, spray with an atomizer or float a few drops on the surface of the drink.

2 oz. Cold-Brew Coffee Concentrate (p. 73)
1 oz. Herbsaint (anise-flavored liqueur)
½ oz. orgeat (almond syrup)
Ice
4 drops of rose water and 1 lemon twist, for garnish

In a cocktail shaker, combine the coffee concentrate, Herbsaint and orgeat. Fill the shaker with ice and shake well. Fine-strain (p. 23) into a chilled, ice-filled wineglass. Garnish with the rose water, then pinch the twist over the drink and add to the glass. —*Nick Detrich*

ISLAY ME DOWN TO SLEEP

MAKES **1 drink**	
BASE **Drambuie**	

"This drink helped me appreciate a nice smoky Scotch," says Atlanta bartender Lindsay Ferdinand. Formerly Scotch-averse, she added some Laphroaig 10-year to a vanilla-infused tea for a superflavorful hot toddy. After steeping the vanilla bean, dry it and add to a jar of sugar to make vanilla sugar.

8 oz. water
1 black tea bag
1 vanilla bean, split lengthwise
1¼ oz. Drambuie (honeyed Scotch-based liqueur)
¼ oz. Islay Scotch, preferably Laphroaig 10-year
1 orange twist, for garnish

In a small saucepan, bring the water to a boil. Add the tea bag and vanilla bean and let steep for 3 to 4 minutes. Discard the tea bag; reserve the vanilla bean for another use. In a warmed heatproof glass or mug, combine the Drambuie, Scotch and 6 oz. of the vanilla-infused tea; stir well. Flame (p. 20) the orange twist over the drink and drop it in. —*Lindsay Ferdinand*

● STRONG ● SWEET ● TART ● BITTER ● FRUITY ● HERBAL ● SMOKY ● SPICY

ITALIAN SUNGLASS MOVIE

MAKES **1 drink**

BASE **Coffee liqueur and Cynar**

New Orleans bartender Nick Detrich loves how easy it is to fix this after-dinner drink. "At home, I can eyeball the pours and just stir with my finger," he says.

¾ oz. coffee liqueur, such as St. George NOLA
¾ oz. Cynar (bitter, artichoke-flavored aperitif)
½ oz. absinthe
2 dashes of orange bitters
1 large ice cube
1 orange twist, for garnish

In a double rocks glass, combine the coffee liqueur, Cynar, absinthe and bitters. Add the ice cube and stir 30 times. Pinch the orange twist over the drink and add to the glass. —*Nick Detrich*

VELVET TELESCOPE

MAKES **1 drink**

BASE **Rum**

"I'm concerned that white grapefruit may be disappearing from the nation's farms," says Nick Detrich, co-owner and bartender at Cane & Table in New Orleans. "So any time I can really highlight grapefruit in a drink, I try to." Here, he combines the fresh juice with coffee-infused rum.

1½ oz. Coffee Rum (below)
¾ oz. fresh white grapefruit juice
½ oz. pineapple gum syrup (available from smallhandfoods.com)
¼ oz. fresh lime juice
7 drops of Peychaud's bitters
Ice cubes, plus crushed ice (p. 23) for serving
1 mint sprig, for garnish

In a cocktail shaker, combine the Coffee Rum, grapefruit juice, gum syrup, lime juice and bitters. Fill the shaker with ice cubes and shake well. Fine-strain (p. 23) into a chilled, crushed ice–filled double rocks glass and garnish with the mint sprig. —*Nick Detrich*

COFFEE RUM
In a jar, combine 8 oz. El Dorado 12-year rum or other aged Demerara rum and ⅓ cup whole coffee beans. Cover and let stand for 20 minutes, shaking the jar every 5 minutes. Strain the infused rum into another jar and keep at room temperature for up to 1 month. Makes 8 oz. —*ND*

HIGH-OCTANE

MAKES **2 drinks**

BASE **Irish cream liqueur**

Cold-brew coffee concentrate does double duty in this cocktail. Lindsay Ferdinand of Atlanta's Common Quarter mixes it with Whisper Creek Tennessee, a whiskey-based cream liqueur. She then serves the drink over a cold-brew coffee ice cube so the flavor doesn't get watered down. Alternatively, you can substitute Buffalo Trace bourbon cream or Baileys Irish cream for the Whisper Creek.

📷 **p. 60**

4 oz. Cold-Brew Coffee Concentrate (below)

3 oz. Irish cream liqueur

1 oz. Fernet-Branca (bitter Italian digestif)

Ice

2 large Cold-Brew Coffee Concentrate ice cubes (below)

2 mint sprigs, for garnish

In a cocktail shaker, combine the Cold-Brew Coffee Concentrate, cream liqueur and Fernet-Branca. Fill the shaker with ice and shake well. Strain into 2 chilled rocks glasses each over a large Cold-Brew Coffee Concentrate ice cube. Smack (p. 23) a mint sprig over each drink and add to the glass. —*Lindsay Ferdinand*

COLD-BREW COFFEE CONCENTRATE

In a large bowl, stir together ⅔ cup coarsely ground coffee beans and 22 oz. cold water. Cover and refrigerate for 12 hours or up to 24 hours for a stronger brew. Line a sieve with cheesecloth and set it over another large bowl. Strain the cold-brew coffee; do not stir the grounds. Pour 3 oz. of the concentrate into each of 2 large ice cube molds and freeze until solid. Pour the remaining concentrate into a jar and refrigerate for up to 1 week. Makes about 10 oz. concentrate and 2 large ice cubes. —*LF*

INCOLD BLOOD
P. 85

FOUR
INGREDIENTS

In the past decade, complicated drinks with dozens of components were so prevalent they became the subject of pop-culture parody. Now, many bartenders are making flavor-packed cocktails with three or four powerhouse ingredients. An added bonus: Guests get their drinks quicker.

BITTER'S BREAKFAST

MAKES **1 drink**

BASE **Amaro**

Whenever New York City bartender Jack Schramm is at a restaurant, he orders an espresso with some type of amaro, a classic Italian after-dinner combo. His trials inspired this chilled interpretation with Bigallet China-China, a bitter orange liqueur.

2 oz. chilled Cold-Brew Coffee Concentrate (p. 73)

1 oz. Amaro Montenegro

¾ oz. Bigallet China-China

1 large ice cube

In a chilled double rocks glass, combine the coffee concentrate, Amaro Montenegro and China-China. Add the ice cube, stir well and serve. —*Jack Schramm*

●●●●●●●●●

SPIRIT ANIMAL

MAKES **1 drink**

BASE **Gin**

Sean Hoard of Teardrop Cocktail Lounge in Portland, Oregon, came up with this drink to pair with bananas Foster for brunch at the Tales of the Cocktail festival in New Orleans. He loves how the caramelized bananas taste with the honeyed flavors in Bénédictine and the peanut-buttery ones in bourbon.

1 oz. gin, preferably Monkey 47 Schwarzwald Dry Gin

½ oz. Bénédictine

½ oz. overproof bourbon, such as Booker's

Ice, plus 1 large cube for serving

1 orange twist, for garnish

In a mixing glass, combine the gin, Bénédictine and bourbon. Fill the glass with ice, stir well and strain into a chilled rocks glass over the large cube. Pinch the orange twist over the drink and add to the glass. —*Sean Hoard*

● STRONG ● SWEET ● TART ● BITTER ● FRUITY ● HERBAL ● SMOKY ● SPICY

BITTER'S
BREAKFAST

DANNY ZUCCA

DANNY ZUCCA

MAKES **1 drink**

BASE **Zucca**

Jack Schramm, head bartender at Booker and Dax in New York City, is a huge fan of amaro, the Italian bitter, herbal digestif. Here, he uses the spiced, rhubarb-flavored Zucca. "I love its bitterness with the sweetness of bourbon," Schramm says.

2 oz. Zucca

1 oz. bonded or overproof bourbon, such as Booker's

¼ oz. fresh lemon juice

2 large ice cubes

In a cocktail shaker, combine the Zucca, bourbon and lemon juice. Add 1 large ice cube and shake well. Strain into a chilled double rocks glass over the remaining large cube.
—*Jack Schramm*

SOUTH OF SUNSET

MAKES **1 drink**

BASE **Gin**

East India sherry, a style of sherry that's rich and sweet, gives this Negroni variation a warm, spiced flavor. The drink is lovely as is, but L.A. bartender Karen Grill also likes it with a dash or two of orange bitters.

1½ oz. gin, preferably Plymouth

¾ oz. Aperol

¾ oz. East India sherry

Ice

1 lemon twist, for garnish

In a mixing glass, combine the gin, Aperol and sherry. Fill the glass with ice and stir well. Strain into a chilled, ice-filled rocks glass. Pinch the lemon twist over the drink and add to the glass.
—*Karen Grill*

● STRONG ● SWEET ● TART ● BITTER ● FRUITY ● HERBAL ● SMOKY ● SPICY

THE LAST ONE

MAKES **1 drink**

BASE **Spanish brandy**

Nico de Soto created this drink for the Experimental Cocktail Club in New York City. "I had to do it again and again to get it right," says de Soto, who is now a co-owner of Mace in Manhattan. He found that shochu, a low-proof Japanese spirit, balanced the intensity of the other ingredients.

1½ oz. Spanish brandy, such as Lustau Brandy de Jerez

¾ oz. Bonal Gentiane-Quina (slightly bitter aperitif wine)

¾ oz. Barolo Chinato

½ oz. sweet potato or carrot shochu, such as Kaikouzu

Ice, plus 1 large cube for serving

In a mixing glass, combine the brandy, Bonal, Chinato and shochu. Fill the glass with ice and stir well. Strain into a chilled rocks glass over the large cube. —*Nico de Soto*

PCM

MAKES **1 drink**

BASE **Pisco**

"There is some rivalry between Peruvian and Chilean pisco distillers, so I wanted to make a cocktail that would bring the two countries together," says Seattle bartender Anu Elford. She combines Peruvian pisco with Chilean Carmenère wine. "In actuality, I might be stirring the pot here. Oh well!"

1½ oz. Peruvian pisco, such as Campo de Encanto

½ oz. fruity red wine, such as Carmenère

¼ oz. buckwheat or other dark honey

Ice

1 lemon twist, for garnish

In a mixing glass, combine the pisco, red wine and honey. Fill the glass with ice and stir well. Strain into a chilled coupe. Pinch the lemon twist over the drink and add to the coupe. —*Anu Elford*

HOLY TRINITY

MAKES **4 drinks**

BASE **Calvados**

Anu Elford, owner of Seattle's Rob Roy, came up with this recipe while sipping lemon ginger tea. This cocktail is actually great hot or cold, especially with the candied ginger garnish for nibbling on.

1 **lemon ginger tea bag**
4 **oz. boiling water**
4 **oz. Calvados**
2 **oz. Pedro Ximénez sherry**
Ice
4 **pieces of candied ginger skewered on picks, for garnish**

1. In a heatproof liquid measuring cup, steep the tea in the boiling water for 4 minutes. Discard the tea bag; refrigerate the brewed tea until chilled, about 1 hour.

2. In a pitcher, combine the chilled tea with the Calvados and sherry. Fill the pitcher with ice and stir well. Strain into chilled coupes. Garnish each drink with a skewered piece of candied ginger. —*Anu Elford*

● STRONG ● SWEET ● TART ● BITTER ● FRUITY ● HERBAL ● SMOKY ● SPICY

FLASHBANG

MAKES **1 drink**	
BASE **Cognac**	

According to Donny Clutterbuck of Cure in Rochester, New York, this drink starts off light, then has a strong finish. "The full effect can be felt after around 10 minutes, and it should take you at least that long to finish it!"

2 oz. overproof Cognac, preferably Louis Royer Force 53

½ oz. Branca Menta (bitter, minty Italian digestif)

½ oz. Bénédictine

Ice

In a cocktail shaker, combine the Cognac, Branca Menta and Bénédictine. Fill the shaker with ice and shake well. Strain into a chilled coupe. —*Donny Clutterbuck*

MEXICAN TRICYCLE

MAKES **1 drink**	
BASE **Mezcal**	

This lightly fizzy, low-proof cocktail is from Andrew Volk, owner and head bartender at Portland Hunt & Alpine Club in Maine. He recommends two to three of these for day drinking, especially on a summer afternoon with good company.

1 oz. mezcal

1 oz. Cynar (bitter, artichoke-flavored aperitif)

Ice

4 oz. chilled dry hard cider

1 lime wheel, for garnish

In a chilled collins glass, combine the mezcal and Cynar. Fill the glass with ice and stir well. Top with the cider and garnish with the lime wheel. —*Andrew Volk*

● STRONG ● SWEET ● TART ● BITTER ● FRUITY ● HERBAL ● SMOKY ● SPICY

FLASHBANG

IN COLD BLOOD

The drink starts with a shot of whiskey (right)

IN COLD BLOOD

MAKES **1 drink**

BASE **Rye whiskey**

Andrew Volk says this is currently the most popular order at Portland Hunt & Alpine Club in Maine. The drink, according to Volk, is "approachable but geeky with the salt"–which he adds to balance the bitterness of the artichoke-flavored aperitif Cynar.

1 oz. rye whiskey, such as Old Overholt

1 oz. Carpano Antica Formula or other sweet vermouth

1 oz. Cynar

1 large ice cube

1 lemon twist and a small pinch of salt (optional), for garnish

In a chilled double rocks glass, combine the whiskey, vermouth and Cynar. Add the large ice cube and stir well. Pinch the lemon twist over the drink and add to the glass. Garnish with the pinch of salt. —*Andrew Volk*

CLINTON + STANTON

MAKES **1 drink**

BASE **Rye whiskey**

Jack Schramm makes a tricked-out version of this cocktail at Booker and Dax in New York City with bran-infused rye, milk-washed apple brandy and a whole egg–a concoction that tastes like a raisin bran milkshake.

1 oz. bonded rye whiskey, preferably Rittenhouse 100 proof

1 oz. bonded apple brandy

1 oz. Pedro Ximénez sherry Cracked ice (p. 23)

In a mixing glass, combine the rye, apple brandy and sherry. Fill the glass with cracked ice and stir well. Strain into a chilled coupe. —*Jack Schramm*

● STRONG ● SWEET ● TART ● BITTER ● FRUITY ● HERBAL ● SMOKY ● SPICY

THE GOOD WORD

MAKES **1 drink**
BASE **Mezcal**

"So many classics are well balanced with just three ingredients, it's quite difficult to come up with a new minimalist drink," says Anu Elford, owner and bartender at Rob Roy in Seattle. She succeeds with this smoky, powerful take on The Last Word.

1½ oz. mezcal
  1 oz. yellow Chartreuse (honeyed herbal liqueur)
½ oz. fresh lemon juice
    Ice, plus 2 large cubes for serving
  1 lemon wedge, for garnish

In a cocktail shaker, combine the mezcal, Chartreuse and lemon juice. Fill the shaker with ice, shake for 5 seconds and strain into a double rocks glass over the 2 large cubes. Garnish with the lemon wedge. —*Anu Elford*

BITTER LIGURIAN

MAKES **1 drink**
BASE **Cognac**

Ezra Star, general manager at Drink in Boston, likes to make this nicely dry cocktail with Pierre Ferrand Ambre, a relatively young and inexpensive Cognac. The drink is also delicious with any good-quality Cognac.

1½ oz. Cognac
1½ oz. Santa Maria al Monte amaro
¼ oz. gum syrup (see Note)
    Ice
  1 orange twist and 1 orange wheel half, for garnish

In a mixing glass, combine the Cognac, amaro and gum syrup. Fill the glass with ice, stir well and strain into a chilled coupe. Pinch the twist over the drink and add to the glass. Garnish with the orange wheel half. —*Ezra Star*

Note Gum syrup, a simple syrup that's been thickened with gum arabic, gives drinks a silky texture; it's available at smallhandfoods.com.

● STRONG ● SWEET ● TART ● BITTER ● FRUITY ● HERBAL ● SMOKY ● SPICY

THE GOOD
WORD

BLASPHEMOUS
RUMORS, P. 94

PAPAYA
CALIENTE
P. 93

PDT/CRIF FROZEN
PIÑA COLADA, P. 90

FROZEN+ SLUSHIE

After years of disrespect, frozen drinks are back in favor. Renowned bartenders are whizzing them in the blender with high-quality spirits and mixers—even running them through slushie machines. Home bartenders will find these drinks very forgiving: To tinker with the ratios, just add a little more spirits or ice and push "blend."

LA PICOSA
P. 97

BLENDER 163 ICED TEA

MAKES **2 drinks**

BASE **Vodka, gin, rum and tequila**

"Bartenders today are applying craft cocktail principles to 'bad' drinks," says John deBary, bar director of the Momo-fuku restaurant empire and chief mixologist for *F&W Cocktails 2016*. At Fuku in Manhattan, deBary uses top-shelf spirits for a terrific slushie version of the much-maligned Long Island Iced Tea.

1 oz. chilled vodka
1 oz. chilled London dry gin
1 oz. white rum
1 oz. blanco tequila
1 oz. Cointreau or other triple sec
1 oz. Simple Syrup (p. 25)
3 cups ice cubes
4 oz. chilled Dr Pepper
2 lime wedges, for garnish

In a blender, combine the vodka, gin, rum, tequila, Cointreau, Simple Syrup and ice and blend until smooth. Pour into 2 chilled double rocks glasses. Stir 2 oz. Dr Pepper into each drink and garnish with the lime wedges. —*John deBary*

PDT/CRIF FROZEN PIÑA COLADA

MAKES **4 drinks**

BASE **Rum**

Jeff Bell of PDT in Manhattan says a piña colada is his guilty-pleasure drink. He makes this superfresh, pineapple-y version in a slushie machine at Crif Dogs, the hot dog joint next to the bar. In place of the typical overly sweetened cream of coconut, Bell blends in coconut water and coconut puree (available frozen at specialty markets).

5 oz. fresh pineapple juice
5 oz. fresh lime juice
3 oz. coconut water
15 oz. chilled white rum, preferably Caña Brava
6 oz. frozen coconut puree, such as Perfect Purée of Napa Valley
3 oz. cane syrup
4 pineapple wedges and 4 cocktail umbrellas (optional), for garnish

Mix the pineapple juice, lime juice and coconut water and pour into an ice cube tray. Freeze until solid, about 4 hours. Transfer the ice cubes to a blender. Add the rum, coconut puree and cane syrup and blend until smooth. Pour into 4 chilled double rocks glasses or large coupes and garnish the drinks with pineapple wedges and cocktail umbrellas. —*Jeff Bell*

●STRONG ●SWEET ○TART ●BITTER ●FRUITY ●HERBAL ●SMOKY ●SPICY

PDT/CRIF FROZEN
PIÑA COLADA

FROZEN
TEA-SCO SOUR

PAPAYA CALIENTE

MAKES	**2 drinks**
BASE	**Rum**

Miami bartender Julio Cabrera re-creates the flavors of *jugo de papaya con anis*, a popular weight-loss drink in the Dominican Republic and Puerto Rico. His rum-laced version here has no purported slimming effects.

📷 p. 88

4 oz. white rum

2 oz. Simple Syrup (p. 25)

1 oz. fresh lime juice

1½ tsp. pastis, preferably Pernod

    Six 1-inch chunks of ripe papaya

2 cups ice cubes

2 tarragon sprigs, for garnish

In a blender, combine the rum, Simple Syrup, lime juice, pastis, papaya and ice and blend until smooth. Pour into 2 large chilled martini glasses and garnish each drink with a tarragon sprig. —*Julio Cabrera*

FROZEN TEA-SCO SOUR

MAKES	**2 drinks**
BASE	**Pisco**

Sam Anderson of Mission Cantina in New York City loves this play on a pisco sour: "Green slushie cocktails make me feel like a kid," he says. The matcha and pisco have a cooling effect that makes the drink a terrific match for the restaurant's fiery Mexican-inspired food.

4 oz. Chilean pisco, such as Capel

2 oz. fresh lime juice

2 oz. Matcha Syrup (below)

1½ cups ice cubes

    2 strawberries, 2 blueberries and 2 blackberries skewered on 2 picks, for garnish

In a blender, combine the pisco, lime juice, Matcha Syrup and ice and blend until smooth. Pour into 2 chilled pilsner or highball glasses and garnish with the skewered berries. —*Sam Anderson*

MATCHA SYRUP

In a heatproof jar, combine ¾ tsp. matcha powder with 8 oz. hot water. Shake until the matcha is dissolved. Add 1 cup sugar and shake until the sugar is dissolved. Let cool and refrigerate for up to 2 weeks. Makes about 12 oz. —*SA*

● STRONG ● SWEET ◗ TART ◒ BITTER ● FRUITY ● HERBAL ● SMOKY ● SPICY

MONKEY TAIL

MAKES **2 drinks**

BASE **Rum**

Micah Melton, beverage director of The Aviary in Chicago, gives this sophisticated frozen daiquiri an ultra-tropical flavor by mixing overproof rum, coconut rum and banana liqueur. To get the right consistency, chill all the ingredients before blending.

1½ oz. chilled overproof Jamaican rum, preferably Wray & Nephew

1½ oz. chilled white rum

1½ oz. chilled fresh orange juice

1½ oz. chilled fresh lime juice

1½ oz. chilled Simple Syrup (p. 25)

1 oz. chilled banana liqueur

1 oz. chilled coconut rum

2 cups ice cubes

In a blender, combine all of the ingredients and blend until smooth. Pour into 2 rocks glasses.

—*Micah Melton*

BLASPHEMOUS RUMORS

MAKES **2 drinks**

BASE **Sherry**

Joaquín Simó, co-owner of Pouring Ribbons in New York City, describes this drink as an even more decadent piña colada. "The bonus," he says, "is that the sherry and Aperol are very low-proof, so the only high-strength ingredient is the bit of green Chartreuse. It's almost responsible–almost." Serve the drink over crushed ice or whiz it in a blender with ice for a slushie version.

📷 p. 88

2 oz. fresh pineapple juice

1½ oz. unsweetened coconut cream

1 oz. Pedro Ximénez sherry

1 oz. East India sherry

1 oz. green Chartreuse (potent herbal liqueur)

1 oz. Aperol

1 oz. fresh lime juice

Crushed ice (p. 23)

2 mint sprigs, 2 star anise pods and 2 pinches of freshly grated nutmeg, for garnish

In a cocktail shaker, combine the pineapple juice, coconut cream, both sherries, the Chartreuse, Aperol and lime juice. Fill the shaker with crushed ice and shake well. Pour into 2 chilled pilsner glasses and garnish each drink with a mint sprig, a star anise pod and a pinch of nutmeg.

—*Joaquín Simó*

● STRONG ● SWEET ● TART ● BITTER ● FRUITY ● HERBAL ● SMOKY ● SPICY

MONKEY
TAIL

LA PICOSA

BANANITA DAIQUIRI

MAKES **2 drinks**

BASE **Rum**

Julio Cabrera has been serving this update on the Cuban classic since day one at The Regent Cocktail Club in Miami. He blends in whole coffee beans to balance out the sweetness of the drink.

4 oz. white rum
1½ oz. banana liqueur
1 oz. fresh lime juice
½ oz. Simple Syrup (p. 25)
2 ripe baby bananas (or 1 regular banana), plus 2 unpeeled banana slices for garnish
4 coffee beans
2 cups ice cubes

In a blender, combine all of the ingredients except the garnish and blend until smooth. Pour into 2 large chilled coupes and garnish each drink with a banana slice. —*Julio Cabrera*

LA PICOSA

MAKES **1 drink**

BASE **Tequila**

The name of this frozen margarita revamp alludes to the drink's flavor (*picosa* means "spicy" in Spanish). Miami bartender Julio Cabrera adds a triple dose of heat with ginger liqueur, jalapeño-infused agave syrup and a cayenne-sugar rim.

2 tsp. sugar
2 tsp. salt
1 tsp. cayenne pepper
1 lime wedge
1½ oz. blanco tequila
½ oz. ginger liqueur, preferably Domaine de Canton
½ oz. Jalapeño Agave Syrup (p. 175)
½ oz. fresh lime juice
1 cup ice cubes

On a small plate, combine the sugar, salt and cayenne. Moisten half of the outer rim of a chilled double rocks glass with the lime wedge and coat lightly with the spice mix. In a blender, combine the tequila, ginger liqueur, jalapeño syrup, lime juice and ice. Blend until smooth and pour into the prepared glass. —*Julio Cabrera*

FROZEN DAISY

MAKES **2 drinks**

BASE **Rum**

Miami bartender Julio Cabrera says this drink is like a frozen mojito with complex, herbal flavors from yellow Chartreuse. The honey-sweetened French liqueur, made with 130 herbs, plants and flowers, dates back to 1838.

3 oz. white rum, preferably
   Bacardí Superior
1 oz. yellow Chartreuse
1 oz. fresh lime juice
1 oz. Simple Syrup (p. 25)
4 dashes of Angostura bitters
2 cups ice cubes
14 mint leaves, plus 2 mint sprigs
   for garnish

In a blender, combine all of the ingredients except the mint sprigs and blend until smooth. Pour into 2 chilled collins glasses and garnish each drink with a mint sprig. —*Julio Cabrera*

KNICKERBOCKER

MAKES **4 to 6 drinks**

BASE **Rum**

Micah Melton, beverage director of The Aviary in Chicago, updates the 1850s classic Knickerbocker–considered to be the great-granddaddy of all tiki drinks. Melton says the best way to enjoy his shocking-pink frozen version is "by the pool in the largest vessel possible."

10 oz. chilled amber rum, such as Zaya 12-year
 9 oz. chilled Raspberry Stock (below)
 7 oz. chilled Simple Syrup (p. 25)
 5 oz. chilled fresh lime juice
 3 oz. chilled Grand Marnier
2½ cups ice cubes

In a blender, combine all of the ingredients and blend until smooth. Pour into chilled rocks glasses. —*Micah Melton*

RASPBERRY STOCK

In a medium saucepan, combine 2 cups raspberries with 8 oz. water and bring to a boil. Remove from the heat, cover and let stand until cooled to room temperature, about 2 hours. Strain the stock into a jar and refrigerate for up to 4 days. Makes about 10 oz. —*MM*

WASABI GRASSHOPPER

MAKES **4 drinks**

BASE **Vodka**

Chicago mixologist Micah Melton gives his grasshopper variation a surprisingly delicious tweak with just a hint of wasabi. He churns batches of the drink in an ice cream maker so it's creamy and smooth, like a thick milkshake.

6 oz. heavy cream
2 Tbsp. sugar
1½ Tbsp. wasabi powder
¼ tsp. salt, plus more for garnish (optional)
4½ oz. white chocolate, chopped
16 oz. skim milk
3 oz. vodka
2 oz. crème de menthe

1. In a small saucepan, bring the cream, sugar, wasabi and ¼ tsp. salt to a simmer over moderately high heat, stirring constantly, about 3 minutes. Whisk in the white chocolate until melted. Remove from the heat and strain the mixture through a fine sieve into a large bowl. Let cool completely, about 30 minutes.

2. Whisk the milk into the mixture, pour into an ice cream maker and freeze according to the manufacturer's instructions. Fold in the vodka. Pour 6 oz. of the grasshopper base into each of 4 chilled double rocks glasses and top each drink with ½ oz. crème de menthe and a pinch of salt. —*Micah Melton*

● STRONG ● SWEET ● TART ● BITTER ● FRUITY ● HERBAL ● SMOKY ● SPICY

MAIDEN NAME, P. 107

TIKI+ TROPICAL

Today's tiki drinks have come a long way since the zombies and mai tais of the '60s. Modern mixologists are focusing on quality spirits, fresh juices and exotic DIY syrups. Some garnish the drinks sparingly while others embrace the kitsch culture of tiki with showy, over-the-top presentations.

TIA MIA

MAKES **1 drink**

BASE **Mezcal and rum**

Ivy Mix, co-owner of Ley-
enda in Brooklyn, riffs on
a mai tai with smoky mez-
cal. The name of the drink
(an anagram of "mai tai")
pays homage to a friend to
whom she used to serve
drinks in Guatemala.

1 oz. mezcal

1 oz. amber rum

¾ oz. fresh lime juice

½ oz. curaçao, preferably Pierre Ferrand Dry

½ oz. orgeat (almond syrup)

  Ice cubes, plus crushed ice (p. 23)
  for serving

1 mint sprig, 1 lime wheel and 1 orchid
  (optional), for garnish

In a cocktail shaker, combine the mezcal, rum,
lime juice, curaçao and orgeat; fill with ice cubes
and shake well. Strain into a chilled, crushed
ice–filled rocks glass. Garnish with the mint sprig,
lime wheel and orchid. —*Ivy Mix*

•••••••••

FEELINGS CATCHER

MAKES **1 drink**

BASE **Bourbon and brandy**

Brooklyn bartender Ivy
Mix gives her nicely bitter
tiki drink a craft cocktail
makeover not just with fresh
juices and high-quality
syrups but also with elite
spirits. She likes to make
Feelings Catcher with Elijah
Craig 12-year bourbon.

¾ oz. bourbon

¾ oz. Spanish brandy, preferably Lustau

½ oz. dark rum

½ oz. guava syrup (available at specialty
  stores and from kalustyans.com)

½ oz. fresh lemon juice

½ oz. fresh grapefruit juice

¼ oz. Cinnamon Syrup (p. 157)
  Crushed ice (p. 23)

2 dashes of Peychaud's bitters

1 mint sprig, for garnish

In a chilled double rocks glass, combine the
bourbon, brandy, rum, guava syrup, lemon juice,
grapefruit juice and Cinnamon Syrup. Fill the
glass with crushed ice. Spin a swizzle stick or
bar spoon between your hands to mix the drink.
Top with more crushed ice. Float the
Peychaud's on top, dashing it over the drink's
surface. Garnish with the mint sprig. —*Ivy Mix*

●STRONG ●SWEET ●TART ●BITTER ●FRUITY ●HERBAL ●SMOKY ●SPICY

TIA MIA

SHORTER,
FASTER,
LOUDER

LITTLE PLASTIC CASTLES

MAKES **1 drink**

BASE **Rum**

Shannon Smith of Porco Lounge and Tiki Room in Cleveland mixes passion fruit syrup with Coco López. The sweet coconut cream, a staple in '80s piña coladas, is having a minor resurgence among today's mixologists. It's part of the recent comeback of retro cocktails.

1½ oz. passion fruit syrup (available at specialty stores and from kalustyans.com)

1½ oz. fresh orange juice

¾ oz. overproof Demerara rum, such as Hamilton 151

¾ oz. amber rum, such as Flor de Caña Añejo

¾ oz. Coco López sweetened cream of coconut

Ice

In a cocktail shaker, combine the passion fruit syrup, orange juice, both rums and Coco López. Fill the shaker with ice and shake well. Pour into a chilled double rocks glass. —Shannon Smith

SHORTER, FASTER, LOUDER

MAKES **1 drink**

BASE **Scotch**

"I love this drink because it's this really weird piña colada variation," says bartender Sara Justice. When guests order it at The Franklin Bar in Philadelphia, she says, "it's fun to see them get excited about a drink that tastes different from the classic flavors they're expecting."

7 basil leaves

1¼ oz. blended Scotch

¼ oz. peated single-malt Scotch, preferably Lagavulin 16-year

¾ oz. Coco López sweetened cream of coconut

½ oz. green Chartreuse (potent herbal liqueur)

½ oz. fresh lemon juice

½ oz. fresh pineapple juice

3 ice cubes, plus crushed ice (p. 23) for serving

Dash of Angostura bitters

1 mint sprig, for garnish

In a cocktail shaker, muddle the basil. Add the Scotches, Coco López, Chartreuse and juices. Add the ice cubes and shake well. Strain into a chilled, crushed ice–filled collins glass. Float the Angostura on top, dashing it over the back of a bar spoon near the drink's surface. Garnish with the mint sprig. —Sara Justice

● STRONG ● SWEET ◐ TART ▣ BITTER ● FRUITY ● HERBAL ● SMOKY ● SPICY

BARBARY BOAT BASIN

MAKES **1 drink**

BASE **Rum**

San Francisco bartender Chad Arnholt recalls the time a chef gave him a handful of Szechuan peppercorns to eat. "My mouth went numb and I almost passed out," Arnholt says. "I guess I was also hooked." He incorporates the notorious mouth-tingling peppercorns in his five-spice syrup here.

1½ oz. white rum
½ oz. overproof rum, preferably Smith & Cross
¾ oz. fresh lime juice
½ oz. Five-Spice Syrup (below)
Dash of Angostura bitters
Ice

In a cocktail shaker, combine both rums, the lime juice, Five-Spice Syrup and bitters. Fill the shaker with ice and shake well. Strain into a chilled rocks glass. —*Chad Arnholt*

FIVE-SPICE SYRUP

In a resealable plastic bag, combine 1 star anise pod, 1¾ tsp. Szechuan peppercorns, ½ tsp. fennel seeds, ½ tsp. whole cloves and one 3-inch cinnamon stick; seal the bag. Using a small, heavy-bottomed saucepan, smash the spices in the bag until coarsely ground. Transfer the spices to the saucepan, add 4 oz. water and bring to a boil over high heat. Remove from the heat and let cool for 10 minutes. Pour the spice syrup through a fine strainer into a large heatproof measuring cup and add enough water to make 4 oz. Stir in 1 cup coconut palm sugar (available at health food stores and markets like Whole Foods); reheat to dissolve if necessary. Let cool, transfer to a jar and refrigerate for up to 2 weeks. Makes about 8 oz. —*CA*

● STRONG ● SWEET ● TART ● BITTER ● FRUITY ● HERBAL ● SMOKY ● SPICY

MAIDEN NAME

MAKES **2 drinks**

BASE **Cachaça**

"Who doesn't like coconut?" asks Ivy Mix of Leyenda in Brooklyn. "I mean, come on, I love piña coladas, but I always want a little more." She gives her version an extra flavor boost with passion fruit syrup, spices and the sugarcane spirit cachaça.

📷 **p. 100**

- **4 oz. cachaça**
- **2 oz. unsweetened coconut cream (alternatively, skim the cream from a can of unsweetened coconut milk)**
- **1 oz. fresh lime juice**
- **1 oz. vanilla syrup (see Note)**
  Generous ½ oz. Cinnamon Syrup (p. 157)
  Generous ½ oz. passion fruit syrup (see Note)
- **3 cups ice cubes**
- **2 small pineapple leaves and freshly grated nutmeg, for garnish**

In a blender, combine the cachaça, coconut cream, lime juice, vanilla syrup, Cinnamon Syrup, passion fruit syrup and ice cubes. Blend until smooth. Pour into 2 chilled tiki mugs or pilsner glasses. Garnish with the pineapple leaves and nutmeg. —*Ivy Mix*

Note Vanilla syrup and passion fruit syrup are both available at specialty stores and from kalustyans.com.

FRENCH AQUATICS

MAKES **1 drink**

BASE **Calvados and Cognac**

Tiki cocktails evoke warm, tropical climates. However, Cleveland bartender Shannon Smith came up with a rich version perfect for the fall with Cognac and apple-inflected Calvados–two brandies that, says Smith, speak to the long history of French ingredients in classic tiki.

2 oz. orgeat (almond syrup)
1 oz. Calvados
1 oz. VS Cognac
1 oz. fresh lime juice
½ oz. overproof Demerara rum, preferably Hamilton 151
½ oz. fresh lemon juice
½ oz. fresh pineapple juice
Ice

In a cocktail shaker, combine all of the ingredients. Fill the shaker with ice and shake well. Pour into a chilled collins glass.
—*Shannon Smith*

IMPERIAL BULLDOG

MAKES **1 drink**

BASE **Aquavit and cachaça**

Imperial Bulldog is the first drink that Jane Danger created with Austin Hennelly, her partner at Mother of Pearl in New York City. She admires his cheeky finishing touches, like the miniature bottle of Underberg bitters inverted in the glass. As the ice melts, the bottle slowly empties into the drink.

5 raspberries, plus 3 raspberries skewered on a pick for garnish
Crushed ice (p. 23)
¾ oz. aquavit
¾ oz. cachaça
¾ oz. fresh lime juice
¾ oz. fresh pineapple juice
¾ oz. Simple Syrup (p. 25)
3 small pineapple leaves and 1 bottle of Underberg bitters (optional), for garnish

In a chilled Belgian beer glass or pilsner glass, muddle the 5 raspberries. Fill with crushed ice. In a cocktail shaker, combine the aquavit, cachaça, lime juice, pineapple juice and Simple Syrup and shake well. Pour into the glass and top with more crushed ice. Garnish with the pineapple leaves and skewered raspberries and invert the bottle of Underberg in the drink.
—*Jane Danger*

● STRONG ● SWEET ● TART ● BITTER ● FRUITY ● HERBAL ● SMOKY ● SPICY

SHARK EYE

FATHER'S ADVICE

MAKES **1 drink**

BASE **Rum**

Ran Duan, owner of The Baldwin Bar outside Boston, makes a nicely dry tiki drink with lots of complexity thanks to a few powerhouse ingredients like sherry and amaro.

1½ oz. amber rum
½ oz. amontillado sherry, preferably Lustau
½ oz. Cardamaro (wine-based amaro)
½ oz. Punt e Mes (spicy, orange-accented Italian sweet vermouth)
¼ oz. banana liqueur
Ice
1 orange twist and 1 brandied cherry skewered on a pick, for garnish

In a mixing glass, combine the rum, sherry, Cardamaro, Punt e Mes and banana liqueur. Fill the glass with ice and stir well. Strain into a chilled coupe. Pinch the orange twist over the drink, skewer it on the pick with the cherry and garnish the drink. —*Ran Duan*

SHARK EYE

MAKES **1 drink**

BASE **Bourbon**

Bourbon and rye give a potent kick to this playful cocktail. At Mother of Pearl in New York City, Jane Danger serves the drink in a shark mug garnished with two thin pineapple fronds arranged to look like a fish. "Shark Eye can make you feel that island vibe on any occasion," Danger says. "Manhattan is an island, right?"

1½ oz. bourbon, preferably Elijah Craig 12-year
¾ oz. passion fruit syrup (available at specialty stores and from kalustyans.com)
¾ oz. fresh lemon juice
½ oz. bonded rye whiskey
¼ oz. Luxardo maraschino liqueur
⅛ oz. curaçao
2 dashes of tiki bitters
Crushed ice (p. 23)
Small pineapple leaves (optional) and 3 dashes of Peychaud's bitters, for garnish

In a cocktail shaker, combine all of the ingredients except the ice and garnishes. Shake well and pour into a chilled, crushed ice–filled shark mug or rocks glass. Garnish with the pineapple leaves and Peychaud's bitters. —*Jane Danger*

● STRONG ● SWEET ● TART ● BITTER ● FRUITY ● HERBAL ● SMOKY ● SPICY

TIDE IS HIGH

MAKES **1 drink**

BASE **Mezcal and tequila**

New York City tiki specialist Jane Danger mixes up this tequila-and-mezcal piña colada variation. Instead of coconut cream, she swaps in homemade cashew cream for a toasty, savory flavor. Alternatively, use store-bought cashew milk, preferably freshly pressed from a juice bar.

1½ oz. unsweetened cashew milk
¾ oz. mezcal
¾ oz. reposado tequila
¾ oz. fresh pineapple juice
½ oz. fresh lime juice
1 tsp. sweetened condensed milk
Crushed ice (p. 23)
3 cashews and 1 orchid (optional), for garnish

In a cocktail shaker, combine all of the ingredients except the ice and garnishes. Shake vigorously and pour into a chilled, crushed ice–filled pilsner glass. Garnish with the cashews and orchid. —*Jane Danger*

DILAPIDATED BEACH HOUSE

MAKES **1 drink**

BASE **Rum**

Espresso meets rum and passion fruit in this modern tiki cocktail that tastes like a boozy, exotic iced coffee. The drink's creator, Shannon Smith of Porco Lounge and Tiki Room in Cleveland, says, "There is something delightful about it both on a sunny patio or in the dead of winter."

1 oz. Trinidadian rum, such as The Scarlet Ibis
1 oz. amber rum
1 oz. Coco López sweetened cream of coconut
1 oz. chilled brewed espresso
½ oz. Cardamaro (wine-based amaro)
½ oz. Cinnamon Syrup (p. 157)
½ oz. passion fruit syrup (available at specialty stores and from kalustyans.com)
Ice
1 orange twist and 1 cocktail umbrella (optional), for garnish

In a cocktail shaker, combine the rums, Coco López, espresso, Cardamaro, Cinnamon Syrup and passion fruit syrup. Fill the shaker with ice and shake well. Pour into a chilled double rocks glass. Pinch the orange twist over the drink and add to the glass. Garnish with the umbrella. —*Shannon Smith*

● STRONG ● SWEET ● TART ● BITTER ● FRUITY ● HERBAL ● SMOKY ● SPICY

TIDE IS
HIGH

THE TALLY MAN
P. 121

HIGH-OCTANE

Complex and potent, high-octane cocktails are meant to be sipped at a leisurely pace. These are the drinks that bartenders fix for themselves and their bartender friends. Boosting their popularity is the increased availability of well-made overproof spirits (at least 50 percent alcohol by volume).

DESK JOB

MAKES **1 drink**
BASE **Rum**

"This drink is like a really bitter, dense rum and Coke–it would be my go-to happy hour cocktail if I had a desk job!" says Donny Clutterbuck, head bartender at Cure in Rochester, New York.

¾ oz. amber rum, preferably Ron Zacapa 23

¾ oz. overproof Jamaican rum, preferably Smith & Cross

¾ oz. Punt e Mes (spicy, orange-accented Italian sweet vermouth)

¾ oz. Cynar (bitter, artichoke-flavored aperitif)

Ice

1 lime twist, for garnish

In a mixing glass, combine the rums, Punt e Mes and Cynar. Fill the glass with ice and stir well. Strain into a chilled, ice-filled rocks glass. Pinch the lime twist over the drink and add to the glass.
—*Donny Clutterbuck*

THREEPENNY OPERA

MAKES **1 drink**
BASE **Fernet-Branca and Campari**

"At some point, every bartender has a love affair with Fernet-Branca and Campari," says Ryan Puckett of the Libertine Liquor Bar in Indianapolis. "I never came out of that phase." He combines the two ingredients in this boozy digestif cocktail, adding a pinch of salt "to open up surprising depth in both spirits."

1 oz. Fernet-Branca (bitter Italian digestif)

1 oz. Campari

1 oz. Carpano Antica Formula or other sweet vermouth

1 oz. curaçao, preferably Pierre Ferrand Dry

Pinch of salt

Ice, plus 1 large cube for serving

1 orange twist, for garnish

In a mixing glass, combine the Fernet-Branca, Campari, Carpano, curaçao and salt. Fill the glass with ice and stir well. Strain into a chilled double rocks glass over the large cube. Pinch the orange twist over the drink and add to the glass.
—*Ryan Puckett*

● STRONG ● SWEET ● TART ● BITTER ● FRUITY ● HERBAL ● SMOKY ● SPICY

DESK JOB

WISE BEYOND HIS YEARS

MAKES **1 drink**

BASE **Scotch**

Jesse Held, bartender at Constantine in Minneapolis, sweetens this smoky Scotch drink with yerba mate–infused honey. Yerba mate, a high-caffeine tea made from a rain forest shrub, has an earthy grassiness that works nicely with Scotch. Leftover yerba mate honey can be used to sweeten tea.

Scant 1 oz. Islay Scotch, preferably Laphroaig cask strength
Scant 1 oz. blended Scotch
½ oz. Licor 43 (citrus-and-vanilla-flavored liqueur)
½ oz. Yerba Mate Honey (below)
½ oz. fresh lemon juice
Dash of orange bitters
4 sage leaves
Ice

In a cocktail shaker, combine the Scotches, Licor 43, Yerba Mate Honey, lemon juice, bitters and 3 of the sage leaves. Fill the shaker with ice and shake well. Fine-strain (p. 23) into a chilled, ice-filled rocks glass. Smack (p. 23) the remaining sage leaf over the drink and add to the glass. —*Jesse Held*

YERBA MATE HONEY

In a medium saucepan, combine 1¼ tsp. loose yerba mate tea, 8 oz. honey and 8 oz. water. Simmer gently over moderately low heat until the honey is melted and the tea leaves are softened, about 15 minutes. Let cool, strain into a jar and refrigerate for up to 2 weeks. Makes about 12 oz. —*JH*

PARLOUR OLD-FASHIONED

MAKES **1 drink**

BASE **Bourbon**

In his quest to make the perfect old-fashioned, Minneapolis bartender Jesse Held concocted this bracing rendition mixed with Mexican brown sugar syrup. "It's strong enough to please the booze-hounds and rich enough for those who want something after dinner."

2 oz. overproof bourbon, such as Booker's
1 oz. rye whiskey
½ oz. Piloncillo Syrup (below)
   Dash of orange bitters
   Dash of Bittercube Cherry Bark Vanilla bitters
   Dash of Angostura bitters
   Ice, plus 1 large cube or ball for serving
1 orange twist and 3 brandied cherries skewered on a pick, for garnish

In a mixing glass, combine the bourbon, rye, Piloncillo Syrup and all of the bitters. Fill the glass with ice and stir well. Strain into a chilled rocks glass over the large cube. Pinch the orange twist over the drink and add to the glass. Garnish with the skewered cherries.
—*Jesse Held*

PILONCILLO SYRUP

In a small saucepan, combine 3 oz. piloncillo (Mexican brown sugar) with 3 oz. water. Simmer over high heat, stirring frequently, until the sugar is dissolved, about 3 minutes. Let cool, strain into a jar and refrigerate for up to 2 weeks. Makes about 4 oz. —*JH*

● STRONG ● SWEET ● TART ● BITTER ● FRUITY ● HERBAL ● SMOKY ● SPICY

ABCDEF

ABCDEF

MAKES **1 drink**

BASE **Gin**

Jeff Bell of PDT in New York City combines six flavor-bomb spirits in this dry, complex cocktail. Each letter in the name stands for an ingredient: B for Beefeater gin, D for Dolin dry vermouth, E for Encanto pisco–and so on.

1½ oz. London dry gin, preferably Beefeater
¾ oz. dry vermouth, preferably Dolin
½ oz. pisco, preferably Encanto
½ oz. Aperol
¼ oz. Campari
¾ tsp. Fernet-Branca (bitter Italian digestif)
Ice

In a mixing glass, combine all of the ingredients. Fill the glass with ice and stir well. Strain into a chilled coupe. —*Jeff Bell*

THE TALLY MAN

MAKES **1 drink**

BASE **Gin**

Indianapolis bartender Ryan Puckett loves to serve this cocktail after dinner "to cleanse the palate and satisfy the sweet tooth." He makes the drink with intensely fragrant Opihr Oriental Spiced gin. If that's not available, swap in another aromatic gin, such as Monkey 47, which is also higher proof.

📷 p. 114

¼ oz. absinthe
2 oz. gin
1 oz. banana liqueur, preferably Giffard Banane du Brésil
4 dashes of lemon bitters
Dash of dark crème de cacao, preferably Tempus Fugit
Ice
1 star anise pod, for garnish

Rinse a chilled coupe with the absinthe; pour out the excess. In a mixing glass, combine the gin, banana liqueur, lemon bitters and crème de cacao. Fill the glass with ice and stir well. Strain into the prepared coupe and garnish with the star anise. —*Ryan Puckett*

WRAY'S NEPHEW

MAKES **1 drink**

BASE **Rum**

Portland, Oregon, bartender Sean Hoard gives this cocktail a potent flavor boost with Wray & Nephew, a 126-proof white rum. In Jamaica, locals use this rum for myriad purifying measures: They rub it on foreheads to prevent colds, sprinkle it on new homes to ward off ghosts and even christen babies with it.

1 oz. overproof rum, preferably Wray & Nephew
½ oz. amber rum
1 oz. fresh pineapple juice
¼ oz. fresh lime juice
¼ oz. Rich Simple Syrup (p. 25)
1 tsp. Fernet-Branca (bitter Italian digestif)
Ice
Pinch of freshly grated nutmeg, for garnish

In a cocktail shaker, combine the rums, juices, Rich Simple Syrup and Fernet-Branca. Fill the shaker with ice and shake well. Strain into a chilled coupe and garnish with grated nutmeg.
—*Sean Hoard*

GOLDEN SLUMBERS

MAKES **1 drink**

BASE **Tequila**

Sean Hoard of Teardrop Cocktail Lounge in Portland, Oregon, uses tequila that's over 100 proof, such as Pueblo Viejo 104, to make this ultrapotent drink. For a tamer version, swap in regular tequila, which is usually between 76 and 80 proof.

1½ oz. overproof tequila
½ oz. Grand Marnier
½ oz. Cocchi Americano (fortified, slightly bitter aperitif wine)
¼ oz. Suze (bittersweet gentian aperitif)
Ice, plus 1 large cube for serving
1 lemon twist, for garnish

In a mixing glass, combine the tequila, Grand Marnier, Cocchi Americano and Suze. Fill the glass with ice and stir well. Strain into a chilled rocks glass over the large cube. Pinch the lemon twist over the drink and add to the glass.
—*Sean Hoard*

KEEN-A ON YOU

MAKES **1 drink**

BASE **Cognac**

"A fervent obsession with the daiquiri/sour formula" spawned this high-octane riff from Donny Clutterbuck, head bartender at Cure in Rochester, New York. Instead of the usual rum, he mixes in overproof Cognac.

1½ oz. overproof Cognac, preferably Louis Royer Force 53 VSOP

¾ oz. fresh lime juice

½ oz. Bigallet China-China (bitter orange liqueur)

½ oz. Simple Syrup (p. 25)

Ice

1 lime twist

In a cocktail shaker, combine the Cognac, lime juice, China-China and Simple Syrup. Fill the shaker with ice and shake well. Fine-strain (p. 23) into a chilled coupe. Pinch the lime twist over the drink and discard. —*Donny Clutterbuck*

PRECARIAT

MAKES **1 drink**

BASE **Bourbon**

"Someone at the bar asked me for a bourbon-based drink that's rich, refreshing and Alpine, and this is what I came up with," says Kyle Linden Webster, co-owner of Expatriate in Portland, Oregon.

1½ oz. overproof bourbon

½ oz. Cocchi Americano (fortified, slightly bitter aperitif wine)

½ oz. Suze (bittersweet gentian aperitif)

½ oz. Dolin Génépy des Alpes (herbal liqueur)

2 dashes of orange bitters

Ice

In a cocktail shaker, combine all of the ingredients. Fill the shaker with ice and shake well. Strain into a chilled coupe. —*Kyle Linden Webster*

● STRONG　● SWEET　● TART　● BITTER　● FRUITY　● HERBAL　● SMOKY　● SPICY

POMME POMME SQUAD

MAKES **1 drink**

BASE **Calvados and Cognac**

"Calvados is having its moment in cocktails, and thank goodness it is!" says Jessica Sanders about the rich apple brandy. The co-owner of Drink.Well and Backbeat in Austin modeled this Sazerac variation on her favorite apple pie recipe. "This drink has all the elements of that incredible pie in liquid form," she says.

- ¼ oz. absinthe
- 1 oz. VSOP Calvados
- 1 oz. overproof Cognac, preferably Louis Royer Force 53 VSOP
- ½ oz. Brown Sugar Syrup (below)
- 2 dashes of Angostura bitters
- 2 dashes of St. Elizabeth allspice liqueur
  Ice
- 1 lemon twist
- 1 dried apple slice, for garnish (optional)

Rinse a chilled snifter with the absinthe; pour out the excess. In a mixing glass, combine the Calvados, Cognac, Brown Sugar Syrup, bitters and allspice liqueur. Fill the glass with ice and stir well. Strain into the prepared snifter. Pinch a lemon twist over the drink and discard. Garnish with the apple slice. *—Jessica Sanders*

BROWN SUGAR SYRUP
In a small saucepan, combine 4 oz. water with ½ cup light brown sugar and bring to a boil. Simmer over moderate heat, stirring frequently, until the sugar is dissolved, about 3 minutes. Let cool, transfer to a jar and refrigerate for up to 1 month. Makes about 6 oz. *—Karen Grill*

● STRONG ● SWEET ● TART ● BITTER ● FRUITY ● HERBAL ● SMOKY ● SPICY

BEYOND THE WALKING DEAD

MAKES **1 drink**

BASE **Rum**

Jesse Held, bartender at Constantine in Minneapolis, created this drink to celebrate the TV show *The Walking Dead*. "I couldn't just make a zombie; I had to make a ZOMBIE!" So he combined four different rums, falernum (a tropical syrup) and fresh juices in a fancy glass with an over-the-top pineapple-cherry garnish. "It may look 'foo foo,' but it will bring the machoest men to their knees," Held says. "I've seen it with my own eyes. It's a buyer-beware kind of cocktail."

1¼ oz. fresh pineapple juice

1 oz. Caribbean white rum

Scant 1 oz. amber rum

Scant 1 oz. overproof rum, preferably Smith & Cross

Scant 1 oz. fresh lime juice

¾ oz. Cinnamon Syrup (p. 157)

½ oz. Velvet Falernum (clove-spiced liqueur)

Dash of tiki bitters

Dash of Bittercube Jamaican #2 bitters or grapefruit bitters

Ice cubes, plus crushed ice (p. 23) for serving

½ oz. dark rum

Pinch of freshly grated nutmeg and 1 brandied cherry skewered on a pick with 1 pineapple slice, for garnish

In a cocktail shaker, combine the pineapple juice, white rum, amber rum, overproof rum, lime juice, Cinnamon Syrup, Velvet Falernum and both bitters. Fill the shaker with ice cubes and shake well. Strain into a chilled, crushed ice–filled tiki mug or pilsner glass and float the dark rum on top, slowly pouring it over the back of a bar spoon near the drink's surface. Garnish with the nutmeg and the skewered cherry and pineapple. *—Jesse Held*

SPANISH HARLEM

MAKES **1 drink**

BASE **Rum**

Austin bartender Jessica Sanders makes this drink with Duque de Carmona Orange dessert wine, but the recipe can be easily replicated by infusing sherry with orange zest. She layers even more orange flavor in the drink with orange bitters and the caramelized essential oils from a flamed orange twist.

¾ oz. overproof rum, preferably Smith & Cross

¾ oz. amber rum

¾ oz. Orange Sherry (below)

½ oz. Date Syrup (below)

4 drops of Bittermens Xocolatl Mole bitters

Dash of orange bitters

Ice

1 orange twist, for garnish

In a mixing glass, combine the rums, Orange Sherry, Date Syrup and both bitters. Fill the glass with ice, stir well and strain into a chilled coupe. Flame (p. 20) the orange twist over the drink and add to the glass. —*Jessica Sanders*

ORANGE SHERRY

Peel strips of zest from half an orange (preferably organic). Transfer the zest to a jar and add 6 oz. oloroso sherry. Cover and let stand for 8 hours at room temperature. Strain the infused sherry into another jar and refrigerate for up to 1 month. Makes 6 oz. —*JS*

DATE SYRUP

In a small saucepan, combine ½ cup chopped dried dates, 1 cup sugar and 8 oz. water. Simmer over moderate heat for 10 minutes. Remove from the heat, cover and let stand for 10 minutes. Let cool, strain into a jar and refrigerate for up to 1 month. Makes about 10 oz. —*JS*

● STRONG ● SWEET ● TART ● BITTER ● FRUITY ● HERBAL ● SMOKY ● SPICY

A FEW SMALL NIPS

MAKES **1 drink**

BASE **Mezcal**

Austin bartender Jessica Sanders took inspiration from a Frida Kahlo painting called *A Few Small Nips* when creating this drink. "Like Frida's great love story with Diego Rivera, this cocktail is fiery and tumultuous but also tender and fragile," she says.

1¼ oz. mezcal
½ oz. pear brandy, such as Clear Creek
¼ oz. yellow Chartreuse (honeyed herbal liqueur)
¼ oz. St-Germain elderflower liqueur
2 dashes of orange bitters
Ice
1 lemon twist, for garnish

In a mixing glass, combine the mezcal, pear brandy, Chartreuse, St-Germain and orange bitters. Fill the glass with ice and stir well. Strain into a chilled coupe. Pinch the lemon twist over the drink and add to the glass.
—*Jessica Sanders*

IMMIGRANT SONG

MAKES **1 drink**

BASE **Rye whiskey**

"Rye whiskey and aquavit may seem like strange bedfellows," says Jessica Sanders, but she finds a tasty way to balance the two spirits. The key, according to Sanders, is to use a whiskey with herbal flavors, like George Dickel.

1¼ oz. rye whiskey
¾ oz. Linie aquavit
½ oz. amontillado sherry
¼ oz. apricot liqueur
2 dashes of celery bitters
Ice
1 lemon twist, for garnish

In a mixing glass, combine the rye, aquavit, sherry, apricot liqueur and bitters. Fill the glass with ice and stir well. Strain into a chilled, ice-filled rocks glass. Pinch the twist over the drink and add to the glass. —*Jessica Sanders*

● STRONG ● SWEET ● TART ● BITTER ● FRUITY ● HERBAL ● SMOKY ● SPICY

WHEN THE
BRITISH CAME TO
SPAIN, P. 139

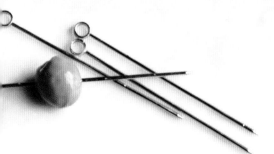

CLASSICS
+RIFFS

Savvy bar goers appreciate a smart tweak on a classic. Delivering a drink that's familiar yet original is a way for mixologists to give guests a singular experience—exactly what people are seeking out these days.

MARTINI
P. 139

MINT JULEP

MINT JULEP

MAKES **1 drink**

BASE **Bourbon**

Kentucky cocktail loyalists say, with straight faces, that when a mint julep is made just right, you can hear angels sing. It's the official drink of the Kentucky Derby–nearly 120,000 mint juleps are served each year at Churchill Downs.

8 mint leaves, plus mint sprigs
  for garnish
½ oz. Simple Syrup (p. 25)
2 oz. bourbon, preferably overproof
  Crushed ice (p. 23)

In a chilled julep cup or fizz glass, muddle the mint leaves and Simple Syrup. Add the bourbon and fill the cup with crushed ice. Spin a swizzle stick or bar spoon between your hands to mix the drink. Top with more crushed ice and garnish with mint sprigs.

ABSINTHE JULEP

MAKES **1 drink**

BASE **Absinthe**

In this mint julep variation, Brooklyn mixologist Maxwell Britten swaps in absinthe for the usual bourbon. After muddling a mint sprig in the cup, he discards it to give the drink just a hint of mint.

2 mint sprigs
1 sugar cube
1 oz. absinthe verte
1 tsp. crème de mûre
  (blackberry liqueur)
1 oz. cold water
  Crushed ice (p. 23)

In a chilled julep cup, muddle 1 of the mint sprigs, then discard. Muddle the sugar cube with the absinthe, crème de mûre and water in the cup and fill with crushed ice. Spin a swizzle stick or bar spoon between your hands to mix the drink. Top with more crushed ice and garnish with the remaining mint sprig. —*Maxwell Britten*

● STRONG ● SWEET ● TART ● BITTER ● FRUITY ● HERBAL ● SMOKY ● SPICY

MANHATTAN

CLASSIC

MAKES **1 drink**

BASE **Rye whiskey**

The legend claiming that the Manhattan was created in New York City for Lady Randolph Churchill doesn't check out. Evidence shows that she was in England at the time, pregnant with the country's future prime minister. It's more likely that the drink was born at the Manhattan Club in the late 19th century.

2 oz. rye whiskey

1 oz. sweet vermouth, preferably Carpano Antica Formula

2 dashes of Angostura bitters
  Ice

1 maraschino cherry, for garnish

In a mixing glass, combine the rye, vermouth and bitters. Fill the glass with ice and stir well. Strain into a chilled coupe and garnish with the cherry.

1910

RIFF

MAKES **1 drink**

BASE **Punt e Mes**

The mezcal in this Manhattan variation from Boston bartender Ezra Star is a clue to deciphering the drink's name—a reference to the year the Mexican Revolution started.

1 oz. Punt e Mes (spicy, orange-accented sweet vermouth)

¾ oz. mezcal

¾ oz. Cognac

½ oz. Luxardo maraschino liqueur

2 dashes of Peychaud's bitters
  Ice

1 orange twist, for garnish

In a mixing glass, combine all of the ingredients except the ice and garnish. Fill the glass with ice, stir well and strain into a chilled coupe. Pinch the orange twist over the drink and add to the coupe. *—Ezra Star*

● STRONG ● SWEET ● TART ● BITTER ● FRUITY ● HERBAL ● SMOKY ● SPICY

1910

SPANISH
RUBY

DAIQUIRI

CLASSIC

MAKES **1 drink**

BASE **Rum**

The daiquiri is named after a beach and iron mine in Santiago, Cuba. It was created by Jennings Cox, an American mining engineer stationed in Cuba during the Spanish-American War. He smartly negotiated a ration of the local white rum as part of his wages.

📷 p. 211

2 oz. white rum
¾ oz. fresh lime juice
¾ oz. Simple Syrup (p. 25)
    Ice
1 lime wheel, for garnish

In a cocktail shaker, combine the rum, lime juice and Simple Syrup. Fill the shaker with ice and shake well. Strain into a chilled coupe and garnish with the lime wheel.

SPANISH RUBY

RIFF

MAKES **1 drink**

BASE **Rum**

Natasha David, co-owner of Nitecap in New York City, makes her daiquiri slightly more complex by adding sherry, cinnamon and bittersweet grapefruit liqueur.

1½ oz. Caribbean white rum, preferably Plantation 3 Stars
1 oz. fresh lime juice
½ oz. amontillado sherry
½ oz. grapefruit liqueur
½ oz. Cinnamon Syrup (p. 157)
    Ice
1 lime wheel, for garnish

In a cocktail shaker, combine the rum, lime juice, sherry, grapefruit liqueur and Cinnamon Syrup. Fill the shaker with ice and shake well. Strain into a chilled coupe and garnish with the lime wheel.
—Natasha David

● STRONG ● SWEET ● TART ● BITTER ● FRUITY ● HERBAL ● SMOKY ● SPICY

●○●●●●●●●

GIN FIZZ

MAKES **1 drink**

BASE **Gin**

The gin fizz, a sour-based cocktail with club soda, was all the rage in the United States until the mid-20th century. This eggless version is the original.

2 oz. London dry gin
¾ oz. fresh lime juice
¾ oz. Simple Syrup (p. 25)
   Ice
1½ oz. club soda
1 maraschino cherry, for garnish

In a cocktail shaker, combine the gin, lime juice and Simple Syrup. Fill the shaker with ice and shake well. Strain into a chilled, ice-filled highball glass, stir in the club soda and garnish with the maraschino cherry.

●○●●●●○●●

DOUBLE-BARREL FIZZ

MAKES **1 drink**

BASE **Rye whiskey**

While most fizz cocktails get their bubbles from seltzer or club soda, Chris Lane tops his drink with sour beer. Lane, bar manager at Ramen Shop in Oakland, California, especially loves Rodenbach Grand Cru, which has a tart fruitiness that's exceptional with his cherry gastrique.

1¾ oz. Rittenhouse 100-proof rye whiskey
¾ oz. fresh lemon juice
¾ oz. Cherry Gastrique (below), plus 3 rehydrated gastrique cherries skewered on a pick for garnish
¼ oz. Cinnamon Syrup (p. 157)
2 dashes of Angostura bitters
   Ice
1½ oz. chilled sour red ale

In a cocktail shaker, combine the whiskey, lemon juice, Cherry Gastrique, Cinnamon Syrup and bitters; fill with ice and shake well. Strain into a chilled, ice-filled double rocks glass. Stir in the ale; garnish with the cherries. —*Chris Lane*

CHERRY GASTRIQUE
In a saucepan, mix 6 oz. tart cherry juice, ¾ cup turbinado sugar, ¾ cup tart dried cherries, 4 oz. white balsamic vinegar and a pinch of salt. Simmer over moderate heat for 10 minutes. Let cool. Strain into a jar; reserve the rehydrated cherries. Refrigerate the gastrique and cherries separately for up to 3 weeks. Makes 8 oz. —*CL*

MARTINI

CLASSIC

MAKES **1 drink**

BASE **Gin**

Despite James Bond's preference, most bartenders will insist that this classic be stirred, not shaken with ice, to prevent it from becoming watered down.

📷 p. 131

3 oz. gin
1 oz. dry vermouth
2 dashes of orange bitters
Ice
1 green olive or 1 lemon twist, for garnish

In a mixing glass, combine the gin, vermouth and bitters. Fill the glass with ice and stir well. Strain into a chilled martini glass or coupe and garnish with the olive or lemon twist.

WHEN THE BRITISH CAME TO SPAIN

RIFF

MAKES **1 drink**

BASE **Gin**

"I'm a big fan of dry martinis," says Ezra Star of Drink in Boston. "I wanted a martini-like drink that was salty and briny." She gives her drink extra flavor with sherry and a rosy tinge with grenadine.

📷 p. 130

1½ oz. Plymouth gin
1 oz. fino sherry
¾ tsp. fresh lemon juice
¾ tsp. grenadine, preferably homemade (p. 25)
¾ tsp. curaçao
¾ tsp. French dry vermouth, such as Dolin
Ice

In a mixing glass, combine all of the ingredients. Fill the glass with ice and stir well. Strain into a chilled coupe. —*Ezra Star*

OLD-FASHIONED

MAKES **1 drink**	
BASE **Bourbon**	

The original recipe for this 19th-century breakfast cocktail called for muddling a sugar cube in the drink. However, many modern bartenders prefer to use simple syrup because it dissolves more easily.

2 oz. bourbon
¼ oz. Rich Simple Syrup (p. 25)
2 dashes of Angostura bitters
Ice
1 orange twist and 1 brandied cherry skewered on a pick, for garnish (optional)

In a mixing glass, combine the bourbon, Rich Simple Syrup and bitters. Fill the glass with ice, stir well and strain into a chilled, ice-filled rocks glass. Pinch the twist over the drink, add it to the glass and garnish with the skewered cherry.

NORSEMAN

MAKES **1 drink**	
BASE **Aquavit**	

Andrew Volk, bartender at Portland Hunt & Alpine Club in Maine, applies the popular mixology technique of fat washing here. He blends browned butter with aquavit, chills the mixture, then scrapes the resolidified butter off the top. The "washed" aquavit takes on the brown butter's nutty flavor without any of the greasiness.

2 oz. Brown Butter–Washed Aquavit (below)
1 tsp. Rich Simple Syrup (p. 25)
2 dashes of Angostura bitters
1 large ice cube
1 apple slice, for garnish

In a chilled double rocks glass, combine the Brown Butter–Washed Aquavit, Rich Simple Syrup and bitters. Add the large ice cube and stir well. Garnish with the apple slice. —*Andrew Volk*

BROWN BUTTER–WASHED AQUAVIT
In a small skillet, cook 3 Tbsp. unsalted butter over moderately low heat until browned, 5 to 7 minutes. Pour through a fine strainer set over a small bowl; let the butter cool. In a jar, combine 8 oz. aquavit with 1 Tbsp. of the brown butter. Let steep at room temperature for 6 to 8 hours, shaking occasionally, then freeze until the fats solidify. Skim off any solids. Refrigerate the brown butter–washed aquavit for up to 4 weeks. Makes about 8 oz. —*AV*

● STRONG ● SWEET ● TART ● BITTER ● FRUITY ● HERBAL ● SMOKY ● SPICY

NORSEMAN

LITTLE
SQUIRT

PALOMA

CLASSIC

MAKES **1 drink**

BASE **Tequila**

Fresca, Squirt and grape-fruit Jarritos are all popular sodas used in this beloved Mexican classic. For a less sweet mixer, try San Pellegrino Pompelmo or a homemade soda (fresh grapefruit juice, seltzer and simple syrup).

📷 p. 179

1 lime wedge and kosher salt
Ice
2 oz. blanco tequila
½ oz. fresh lime juice
2 oz. chilled grapefruit soda
1 grapefruit wheel half, for garnish

Moisten the outer rim of a chilled highball glass with the lime wedge; coat lightly with salt. Fill the glass with ice. In a cocktail shaker, combine the tequila and lime juice. Fill with ice, shake well and strain into the prepared glass. Stir in the grapefruit soda and garnish with the grapefruit.

LITTLE SQUIRT

RIFF

MAKES **1 drink**

BASE **Tequila**

Jeff Bell of PDT in New York City makes this savory take on a paloma with red bell pepper. He amps up the pepper flavor with a salty rim that includes four kinds of peppercorns. For an easy shortcut, look for bottles of mixed peppercorns with built-in grinders.

¼ tsp. each ground green, white, black and pink peppercorns (or 1 tsp. ground pepper from a premixed peppercorn medley)
4 tsp. kosher salt
1 lime wedge
Ice
One 1-inch square of red bell pepper
1½ oz. blanco tequila
¾ oz. yellow Chartreuse (honeyed herbal liqueur)
¾ oz. fresh lemon juice
¼ oz. mezcal
1½ oz. chilled Squirt or other grapefruit soda

On a small plate, mix the ground pepper and salt. Moisten the outer rim of a chilled collins glass with the lime wedge; coat lightly with the spice salt. Fill the glass with ice. In a cocktail shaker, muddle the bell pepper. Add the tequila, Char-treuse, lemon juice and mezcal. Fill the shaker with ice, shake well and fine-strain (p. 23) into the prepared glass. Stir in the Squirt. *—Jeff Bell*

● STRONG ● SWEET ● TART ● BITTER ● FRUITY ● HERBAL ● SMOKY ● SPICY

HOMEMADE EGGNOG

MAKES **10 drinks**

BASE **Bourbon**

Eggnog is usually spiked with brandy, rum or bourbon. This not-too-rich version includes all three. Salt accents the spirits and helps cut the drink's richness.

- 6 **large eggs, separated**
- ¾ **cup sugar**
- 24 **oz. milk**
- 8 **oz. bourbon**
- 4 **oz. dark rum**
- 4 **oz. brandy**
- 8 **oz. heavy cream**
- ½ **tsp. freshly grated nutmeg**
  Salt, for garnish (optional)

1. Put the egg yolks in a large bowl and set the bowl over a saucepan of simmering water. Add half of the sugar and whisk over low heat until pale yellow and thick, about 5 minutes. Whisk in the milk, bourbon, rum and brandy.

2. In another large bowl, whisk the egg whites with the remaining sugar until very soft peaks form. Stir the whites into the yolk mixture. In a medium bowl, beat the heavy cream until lightly thickened. Fold the whipped cream and nutmeg into the eggnog and refrigerate until thoroughly chilled, about 2 hours. Whisk to reblend, then pour into chilled coupes and garnish each drink with a pinch of salt.

ABSINTHE EGGNOG

MAKES **4 drinks**

BASE **Absinthe**

Brooklyn mixologist Maxwell Britten is an absinthe obsessive. Here, he features the anise-flavored spirit in eggnog. For the recipe, Britten prefers a Swiss white absinthe, such as La Clandestine, which tends to be milder than the green varieties.

EGGNOG

- **3 large eggs, separated, plus 1 large egg yolk**
- **¼ cup plus 1 Tbsp. sugar**
- **16 oz. whole milk**
- **4 oz. heavy cream**
- **1½ tsp. pure vanilla extract**
- **¼ tsp. freshly grated cinnamon**
- **⅛ tsp. salt**

COCKTAIL

- **13 oz. chilled eggnog (above) or store-bought eggnog**
- **3 oz. chilled absinthe**
- **4 pinches of salt**
- **Freshly grated nutmeg, for garnish**

1. Make the eggnog In a large bowl, beat the egg whites with a hand mixer until stiff peaks form. Gently fold in ¼ cup of the sugar. In a medium bowl, beat the 4 yolks until combined. Fold the yolks into the whites, then stir in the milk, cream, vanilla, cinnamon, salt and the remaining 1 Tbsp. of sugar. Transfer the eggnog to an airtight container and refrigerate until thoroughly chilled, about 2 hours.

2. Make the cocktail In a pitcher, combine 13 oz. of the eggnog with the absinthe and salt. Stir well and fine-strain (p. 23) into chilled coupes. Garnish each drink with nutmeg.
—*Maxwell Britten*

● STRONG ● SWEET ● TART ● BITTER ● FRUITY ● HERBAL ● SMOKY ● SPICY

PISCO SOUR

●●●●●●●●●●

CLASSIC

MAKES **1 drink**

BASE **Pisco**

The pisco sour is a whiskey sour variation invented in Lima, Peru. Preshaking the drink without ice emulsifies the egg white and gives the drink an airy texture.

2 oz. pisco
¾ oz. fresh lime juice
¾ oz. Simple Syrup (p. 25)
1 large egg white
Ice
4 drops of Angostura bitters, for garnish

In a cocktail shaker, combine the pisco, lime juice, Simple Syrup and egg white and shake vigorously. Fill the shaker with ice and shake again. Strain into a chilled coupe. Dot the drink with the bitters and draw a toothpick through the drops to swirl decoratively.

●●●●●●●●●

SALAD DAYS SOUR

RIFF

MAKES **1 drink**

BASE **Pisco**

Derek Brown of Mockingbird Hill in Washington, DC, gives his pisco sour a savory spin with celery-infused pisco. He then burns ground cinnamon to sprinkle on the drink. "I've always had trouble with cinnamon on things," he says. "It makes me want to cough, but not when it's burnt." Brown garnishes the drink with bits of raw carrot. Alternatively, you can add crisp, dehydrated carrot chips.

1½ oz. Celery Pisco (below)
¾ oz. fresh lemon juice
¾ oz. Rich Simple Syrup (p. 25)
1 large egg white
Ice
⅛ tsp. ground cinnamon and carrot chips (optional), for garnish

1. In a cocktail shaker, combine the Celery Pisco, lemon juice, Rich Simple Syrup and egg white and shake vigorously. Fill the shaker with ice and shake again. Strain into a chilled coupe.

2. In a small heatproof bowl, use a lighter or long match to ignite the cinnamon and let it smolder. Garnish the drink with the carrot chips and a pinch of the cinnamon ash. —Derek Brown

CELERY PISCO

In a jar, combine ⅓ cup chopped celery and 8 oz. Peruvian pisco, such as Encanto. Let steep overnight. Strain into another jar; refrigerate for up to 2 weeks. Makes 8 oz. —DB

● STRONG ● SWEET ● TART ● BITTER ● FRUITY ● HERBAL ● SMOKY ● SPICY

PISCO SOUR

TINGLING NEGRONI

NEGRONI

MAKES **1 drink**

BASE **Gin**

The Negroni's unmistakable bittersweet flavor has spawned countless drink and non-drink interpretations. These include Negroni pie, Negroni pizza–even Negroni lip balm.

📷 p. 212

1 oz. gin, preferably London dry
1 oz. Campari
1 oz. sweet vermouth
Ice
1 orange twist, for garnish

In a mixing glass, combine the gin, Campari and vermouth; fill with ice and stir well. Strain into a chilled coupe; pinch the orange twist over the drink and add to the glass. Alternatively, strain into a chilled, ice-filled rocks glass and garnish.

TINGLING NEGRONI

MAKES **1 drink**

BASE **Gin**

"I wanted to do a Negroni unlike any other," says Sam Anderson, head bartender at Mission Chinese Food in New York City. In place of the traditional sweet vermouth, he stirs in pine fruit liqueur (pine fruit matures into a pinecone). Anderson then adds a few drops of numbing Sichuan peppercorn oil "for a whiff of strange."

1 oz. London dry gin
1 oz. Aperol
½ oz. Cynar (bitter, artichoke-flavored aperitif)
½ oz. Zirbenz Stone Pine Liqueur of the Alps
Ice
4 drops of Sichuan Peppercorn Oil (below)
1 rosemary sprig, for garnish

In a mixing glass, combine the gin, Aperol, Cynar and pine liqueur; fill with ice and stir well. Strain into a chilled, ice-filled rocks glass. Dot the peppercorn oil over the surface of the drink and garnish with the rosemary sprig. —Sam Anderson

SICHUAN PEPPERCORN OIL

In a spice grinder, coarsely grind 2 tsp. Sichuan peppercorns. In a small saucepan, combine the ground peppercorns with ¼ cup peanut oil and cook over moderate heat, swirling occasionally, until the peppercorns darken, about 1 minute. Let cool, then pour into a jar. Refrigerate for up to 3 months. Bring to room temperature and stir before using. Makes ¼ cup.

COLONIAL
HEIRLOOM
P. 162

LARGE-FORMAT

Punches, pitcher drinks, cocktails on tap–these big-batch libations are all going strong at bars. Now that it's easier to source huge ice blocks, mixologists can hand-carve them for dramatic presentations. Another reason for the prevalence of large-format cocktails: They're easy to make for groups, both in bars and at home.

EVERYTHING'S
COMING UP ROSÉ

THE MODEL U.N.

MAKES **3 to 4 drinks**

BASE **Japanese whisky**

Chicago mixologist Jacyara de Oliveira gives her Japanese punch an unexpected British twist with single-malt Islay Scotch. Islay, an island off the coast of Scotland, tends to produce the smokiest whiskies, with flavors that can be as challenging as their unpronounceable names.

6 oz. 12-year Japanese whisky

4 oz. water

3 oz. Matcha Syrup (p. 93)

2 oz. fresh lime juice

1 oz. single-malt Islay Scotch, preferably Laphroaig

1 oz. yuzu juice (see Note)

Ice

In a pitcher, combine the whisky, water, Matcha Syrup, lime juice, Scotch and yuzu juice. Add ice and stir well. Strain into an ice-filled punch bowl and serve in chilled rocks glasses.
—*Jacyara de Oliveira*

Note If fresh yuzu isn't available, look for bottled yuzu juice at Japanese markets.

EVERYTHING'S COMING UP ROSÉ

MAKES **4 to 6 drinks**

BASE **Rosé**

Natasha David, co-owner of Nitecap in New York City, creates this sophisticated sangria by combining rosé wine with pleasantly bitter Aperol and delicate, floral hibiscus tea.

8 oz. chilled dry rosé

4 oz. Lillet rosé

4 oz. chilled brewed hibiscus tea

2 oz. fresh lemon juice

2 oz. Simple Syrup (p. 25)

1 oz. Aperol

Ice

4 oz. chilled club soda

Grapefruit wheel halves, lemon wheels and sliced strawberries, for garnish

In a pitcher or punch bowl, combine the rosé, Lillet, tea, lemon juice, Simple Syrup and Aperol. Fill the pitcher with ice and stir well. Stir in the club soda and garnish with the fruit. Serve in chilled wineglasses. —*Natasha David*

CARIBBEAN FAIRY

MAKES **6 drinks**

BASE **Absinthe**

"This is seriously the friendliest absinthe drink I've ever had!" says Houston bar impresario Bobby Heugel. "Everyone loves it despite strong opinions on licorice flavors." He serves this creamy but not-too-rich cocktail in young coconut shells and encourages scraping up the coconut flesh with a spoon.

18 oz. coconut water
6 oz. absinthe
4 oz. sweetened condensed milk
Crushed ice (p. 23)
Freshly grated nutmeg and mint leaves, for garnish
6 young coconut shells, for serving (optional)

In a pitcher, stir the coconut water with the absinthe and condensed milk until fully combined. Pour into a punch bowl filled with crushed ice. Garnish with the nutmeg. Smack (p. 23) the mint leaves over the drink and add to the bowl. Ladle into crushed ice–filled coconut shells or chilled, crushed ice–filled rocks glasses. —*Bobby Heugel*

•••••••••

STAY GOLDEN

MAKES **8 drinks**

BASE **Pisco**

"In the early days of punch houses," says Chicago bartender Jacyara de Oliveira, "groups would mingle over a bowl and discuss news, politics and the day-to-day." In keeping with that tradition, she created a pisco-tea punch that's flavorful yet not too strong. "It will get you buzzed, for sure, but allow you to keep up a witty repartee."

2 black tea bags
2 oz. honey
8 oz. pisco
4 oz. Cocchi Vermouth di Torino
2 oz. yellow Chartreuse (honeyed herbal liqueur)
2 oz. fresh lemon juice
Ice
Lemon wheels and thyme and mint sprigs, for garnish

1. In a large heatproof measuring cup, steep the tea bags in 16 oz. of hot water for 4 minutes. Discard the tea bags; stir in the honey and refrigerate until chilled, about 2 hours.

2. In a pitcher, combine 12 oz. of the tea with the pisco, vermouth, Chartreuse and lemon juice; add ice and stir well. Pour into chilled rocks glasses and garnish. —*Jacyara de Oliveira*

● STRONG ● SWEET ○ TART ● BITTER ● FRUITY ● HERBAL ● SMOKY ● SPICY

CARIBBEAN
FAIRY

ST. HENRY PUNCH

MAKES **4 drinks**

BASE **Gin**

Green melon in cocktails can be cloying, as anyone who's had too many Midori sours can tell you. In this lovely floral gin punch, Sean Kenyon, co-owner of Williams & Graham in Denver, tames the sweetness of honeydew juice with jasmine green tea and lemon juice.

2 jasmine green tea bags

3 oz. hot water

Crushed ice (p. 23) and ice cubes, plus a large block of ice (p. 23) for serving

8 oz. London dry gin

4 oz. fresh honeydew melon juice

3½ oz. Simple Syrup (p. 25)

3 oz. fresh lemon juice

2 oz. ginger liqueur

2 dashes of Angostura bitters

1 slice of honeydew melon, for garnish

1. In a heatproof measuring cup, steep the tea bags in the hot water for 3 minutes, then discard the tea bags. Add crushed ice until the brewed tea measures 6 oz. Let the ice melt and the tea cool completely.

2. In a pitcher, combine the tea, gin, melon juice, Simple Syrup, lemon juice, ginger liqueur and bitters. Add ice cubes and stir well. Strain into a punch bowl over the large block of ice and garnish with the melon slice. Ladle into chilled punch cups or rocks glasses. —*Sean Kenyon*

ZIGGY STARDUST

MAKES **4 drinks**

BASE **Rum**

Natasha David of Nitecap in New York City creates a punch versatile enough for all seasons. "Rum and lime juice are a classic summertime favorite," she says, "while cinnamon warms it up a bit."

6 oz. white rum

3 oz. fresh lime juice

2 oz. amontillado sherry

2 oz. Cinnamon Syrup (below)

1 oz. peach liqueur

½ oz. fresh orange juice

Ice cubes, plus a large block of ice (p. 23) for serving

4 oz. chilled dry sparkling wine

Lime wheels, orange wedges and freshly grated or ground cinnamon, for garnish

In a medium bowl, combine the rum, lime juice, sherry, Cinnamon Syrup, peach liqueur and orange juice. Add the ice cubes and "roll" the drink by pouring it back and forth several times between 2 bowls. Strain into a punch bowl over the large block of ice and stir in the sparkling wine. Garnish with lime wheels, orange wedges and cinnamon and ladle into rocks glasses. —*Natasha David*

CINNAMON SYRUP

In a medium saucepan, combine 16 oz. water with 2 cups sugar and 6 medium cinnamon sticks. Stir over moderate heat until the sugar is dissolved, then simmer (do not boil) for 10 minutes. Let cool. Remove the cinnamon sticks and pour the syrup into a jar. Refrigerate for up to 2 weeks. Makes about 24 oz. —*ND*

● STRONG ● SWEET ● TART ● BITTER ● FRUITY ● HERBAL ● SMOKY ● SPICY

APPELLATION
COOLER

APPELLATION COOLER

MAKES **4 to 6 drinks**	
BASE **White wine**	

"I want to give the white wine spritzer its rightful place in the cocktail world," says New York City bartender Natasha David. She upgrades the oft-diluted, lightweight drink with basil-infused vermouth and Cocchi Americano, a bitter aperitif wine. Her pro tip: "Make sure to eat those punch-soaked cucumber slices!"

8 oz. dry white wine, preferably Muscadet
4 oz. Cocchi Americano
4 oz. Basil Vermouth (below)
4 tsp. apricot liqueur, preferably Rothman & Winter Orchard Apricot
Ice
4 oz. chilled dry sparkling wine
Seedless cucumber slices, for garnish

In a pitcher, combine the wine, Cocchi Americano, Basil Vermouth and apricot liqueur. Fill the pitcher with ice and stir well. Stir in the sparkling wine and garnish with the cucumber slices. Serve in chilled white wine glasses.
—Natasha David

BASIL VERMOUTH
In a jar, combine 1 cup loosely packed basil sprigs with 8 oz. Dolin blanc vermouth. Cover and let stand for 1 hour. Strain into another jar and refrigerate for up to 2 weeks. Makes 8 oz. —ND

FRENCHED HOT CHOCOLATE

MAKES **3 to 4 drinks**

BASE **Chartreuse**

"Chartreuse and chocolate is among the world's most underrated combinations," says Bobby Heugel, co-owner of Anvil Bar & Refuge in Houston. He melds the two ingredients in this boozy, rich hot chocolate.

12 oz. whole milk

6 oz. yellow Chartreuse (honeyed herbal liqueur)

4 oz. Calvados

2 oz. dark chocolate, chopped

1 vanilla bean, split lengthwise and seeds scraped

One 3-inch cinnamon stick, plus freshly grated or ground cinnamon for garnish

In a medium saucepan, combine the milk, Chartreuse, Calvados, chocolate, vanilla bean and seeds and cinnamon stick. Stir constantly over moderate heat until the chocolate is completely melted. Remove from the heat, discard the vanilla bean and whisk the hot chocolate until frothy. Ladle into warmed mugs or heatproof glasses and garnish with cinnamon.

—*Bobby Heugel*

● STRONG ● SWEET ● TART ● BITTER ● FRUITY ● HERBAL ● SMOKY ● SPICY

FRENCHED HOT
CHOCOLATE

COLONIAL HEIRLOOM

MAKES **8 drinks**

BASE **Gin and Batavia-Arrack**

Houston bartender Bobby Heugel riffs on Bombay Government Punch, a recipe from the early colonial era of India. He adds Earl Grey tea and kaffir lime leaves to his oleo-saccharum—a mix of citrus oil and sugar that many bartenders consider an indispensable ingredient in punches.

📷 **p. 150**

8 oz. chilled brewed Earl Grey tea

4 oz. fresh lime juice

Herbed Oleo-Saccharum (below)

8 oz. London dry gin

8 oz. Batavia-Arrack van Oosten (spicy, citrusy rum-like spirit)

Ice

8 oz. chilled club soda

Lime wheels, rosemary sprigs and kaffir lime leaves, for garnish

1. In a bowl, combine the tea and lime juice with the oleo-saccharum and stir to dissolve. Strain the liquid into a punch bowl.

2. Add the gin and Batavia-Arrack to the punch bowl, fill with ice and stir well. Stir in the club soda and garnish with lime wheels, rosemary sprigs and lime leaves. Serve in chilled punch cups or rocks glasses. —*Bobby Heugel*

HERBED OLEO-SACCHARUM

Using a vegetable peeler, remove the zest in strips from 2 lemons and 2 limes, preferably organic. Transfer the zests to a shallow medium bowl; add 4 kaffir lime leaves and 2 rosemary sprigs. Add 1 cup sugar and muddle the ingredients until the zests begin to release their oils. Push the zests to the sides of the bowl, cover and let macerate overnight. Refrigerate for up to 2 weeks. —*BH*

SILK CITY PUNCH

MAKES **5 drinks**

BASE **Bourbon**

The esteemed cocktail historian David Wondrich once told Denver bartender Sean Kenyon that every great punch tastes like delicious iced tea or lemonade. "This one tastes like a refreshing peach tea," Kenyon states.

2 Earl Grey tea bags

6 oz. hot water

Crushed ice (p. 23), plus cubes for serving

6 oz. bourbon

3 oz. amber rum, preferably Ron Zacapa 23

3 oz. Simple Syrup (p. 25)

2 oz. peach liqueur

2 oz. fresh lemon juice

5 lemon wheels, for garnish

1. In a large heatproof measuring cup, steep the tea bags in the hot water for 4 minutes, then discard the tea bags. Add crushed ice until the brewed tea measures 9 oz. Let the ice melt and the tea cool completely.

2. In a pitcher, combine the tea, bourbon, rum, Simple Syrup, peach liqueur and lemon juice. Add ice cubes and stir well. Strain into a punch bowl over ice cubes and garnish with the lemon wheels. Ladle into chilled punch cups or rocks glasses. —*Sean Kenyon*

● STRONG ● SWEET ● TART ● BITTER ● FRUITY ● HERBAL ● SMOKY ● SPICY

CHASING
SUMMER, P. 170

MOCKTAILS

More and more bars are devoting entire sections of their menus to nonalcoholic drinks. The new mocktails aren't necessarily trying to taste like cocktails; they stand on their own, especially as bartenders get more creative in sourcing fascinating and complex ingredients.

ECTO CHELADA

MAKES **8 drinks**

BASE **Vegetable juice**

"I bought a fancy juicer just to make this," says Chad Arnholt, bartender at Comstock Saloon in San Francisco. "The savory ingredients—cucumbers, peppers, herbs—are unexpected and make the drink feel healthy." He sets out a pitcher of the juice for parties, cookouts or sci-fi movie nights along with tequila, beer and ginger beer so guests can customize their own drinks.

4 tsp. togarashi (a Japanese spice blend of chiles and sesame)

2 tsp. kosher salt

1 lime wedge

24 oz. chilled ginger beer or ginger ale

24 oz. Green Juice Blend (below)

Ice

1. On a small plate, combine the togarashi and salt. Moisten the outer rims of 8 chilled collins glasses with the lime wedge and coat lightly with the spice mix.

2. In each prepared glass, combine 3 oz. ginger beer with 3 oz. Green Juice Blend. Fill each glass with ice and stir well. —*Chad Arnholt*

GREEN JUICE BLEND

In a juicer, juice 1 bunch of mint, 1 bunch of dill and 1 seeded jalapeño with 3 to 4 green apples to yield 17 oz. of juice. Transfer to a pitcher and add 10 oz. fresh green or yellow tomato juice, 8 oz. fresh cucumber juice and 2 oz. fresh lime juice. Add 1 tsp. kosher salt and stir well. Makes about 37 oz. —*CA*

ECTO
CHELADA

PHILIPPE
KHALLINS

PHILIPPE KHALLINS

MAKES **2 drinks**

BASE **Coconut milk**

At Mission Chinese Food in New York City, Sam Anderson mixes coconut milk with gin and serves the drink in small soup bowls because the flavors are reminiscent of Thai tom kha gai soup. This mocktail variation is rich, creamy and incredibly aromatic.

10 oz. Coconut Mix (below)
2 oz. fresh pineapple juice
1 oz. fresh lime juice
Ice
2 kaffir lime leaves and a sprinkle of cayenne pepper, for garnish

In a cocktail shaker, combine the Coconut Mix, pineapple juice and lime juice. Fill the shaker with ice and shake well. Strain into 2 chilled tea cups and add a few ice cubes. Garnish with the lime leaves and cayenne pepper.
—Sam Anderson

COCONUT MIX

In a medium saucepan, combine one 13⅔-oz. can unsweetened coconut milk, ½ cup plus 2 Tbsp. sugar, ¼ cup minced fresh ginger, 2 Tbsp. thinly sliced fresh lemongrass, 1½ small dried Tianjin (Chinese red) chiles and ¼ tsp. salt. Cook over moderate heat until simmering, 2 to 3 minutes. Remove from the heat and add ¼ cup kaffir lime leaves. Let cool, transfer to a jar and refrigerate overnight. Strain through a cheesecloth-lined sieve into another jar and refrigerate for up to 1 week. Makes about 13 oz. —SA

● STRONG ● SWEET ● TART ● BITTER ● FRUITY ● HERBAL ● SMOKY ● SPICY

EARLY BIRD

MAKES **1 drink**

BASE **Coffee**

Indianapolis bartender Ryan Puckett relies on this drink as his morning eye-opener. "It came out of necessity and a mighty hangover," he admits. For the cold-brew coffee, Puckett prefers a nitrogen-infused coffee "that sends you into hyper speed." The recipe here calls for conventional cold-brew.

2 orange twists
3 oz. Cold-Brew Coffee Concentrate (p. 73)
¾ oz. orgeat (almond syrup)
¼ to ½ oz. Simple Syrup (p. 25)
1 large egg white
Ice

In a cocktail shaker, muddle the orange twists. Add the coffee concentrate, orgeat, Simple Syrup and egg white and shake vigorously. Fill the shaker with ice and shake again. Strain the drink into a chilled coupe. —*Ryan Puckett*

CHASING SUMMER

MAKES **1 drink**

BASE **Chai tea**

"I love this drink so much that it seems like my glass is always empty," says Lacy Hawkins, bartender at The NoMad in New York City. Her favorite part is the balsamic vinegar. "It adds wonderful acidity to the drink and creates a caramelized finish."

📷 p. 164

4 oz. Chai Sun Tea (below)
¾ oz. passion fruit puree or juice
½ oz. sweetened condensed milk
¼ oz. balsamic vinegar
Ice cubes, plus crushed ice (p. 23) for serving

In a cocktail shaker, combine the Chai Sun Tea, passion fruit puree, condensed milk and vinegar. Fill the shaker with ice cubes and shake well. Strain into a chilled, crushed ice–filled collins glass. —*Lacy Hawkins*

CHAI SUN TEA
Place 1 chai tea bag and 12 oz. cold water in a glass jar. Cover and leave in a sunny, warm place for 1 hour. Discard the tea bag and refrigerate the tea for up to 2 weeks. Makes 12 oz. —*LH*

SALTED LIME RICKEY

MAKES **1 drink**

BASE **Cherry juice**

Inspired by Vietnamese-style salted limeade, Ran Duan, owner of The Baldwin Bar outside Boston, revamps a soda fountain throwback. He says the drink is easily adaptable to other fruits, sweeteners and spices like cardamom and vanilla.

5 pitted Bing cherries
½ lime, cut into wedges
1 Tbsp. sugar
Pinch of salt
Ice
4 oz. chilled club soda

In a cocktail shaker, muddle the cherries with the lime wedges, sugar and salt. Fill the shaker with ice and shake well. Strain into a chilled, ice-filled highball glass and stir in the club soda. —*Ran Duan*

EXTENDED SESSION

MAKES **2 drinks**

BASE **Black tea**

Chicago bartender Jacyara de Oliveira likes to make this spiced iced tea punch in a coffee press to strain out the citrus wheels and star anise. You could also make the drink in a pitcher and pour it through a strainer before serving.

(Most bitters are alcohol-based. For a completely nonalcoholic cocktail, leave them out.)

4 oz. chilled brewed black tea
4 oz. verjus (see Note)
2 oz. Honey Syrup (p. 25)
½ oz. lemon juice
½ oz. cardamom bitters
¼ oz. Angostura bitters
Ice
2 lemon wheels, 2 orange wheels and 2 star anise pods

In a large coffee press or small pitcher, combine the tea, verjus, Honey Syrup, lemon juice and both bitters. Fill the press with ice and stir well. Add the citrus wheels and star anise. To serve, push down the plunger of the coffee press and strain the drink into rocks glasses.
—*Jacyara de Oliveira*

Note Verjus, the tart juice pressed from unripe grapes, is available at specialty food stores.

● STRONG ● SWEET ○ TART ● BITTER ● FRUITY ● HERBAL ● SMOKY ● SPICY

COCO LOCO

MAKES **1 drink**

BASE **Orange soda**

Indianapolis bartender Ryan Puckett combines his penchant for tiki cocktails with a childhood favorite, orange soda floats; the result is this tropical orange-cream soda. "I'd make orange soda floats with my grandma, so that flavor pairing is something I've always loved," he says.

1 oz. Coco López sweetened cream of coconut
1 oz. heavy cream
1 oz. fresh pineapple juice
   Ice
4 oz. chilled orange soda, such as San Pellegrino Aranciata
   Small pinch of freshly grated nutmeg, for garnish

In a cocktail shaker, combine the Coco López, cream and pineapple juice. Fill the shaker with ice and shake well. Pour the soda into a chilled, ice-filled collins glass; strain the contents of the shaker into the glass and garnish with the nutmeg. —*Ryan Puckett*

CHAMOMILE LEMONADE

MAKES **1 drink**

BASE **Lemonade**

Devon Tarby, co-owner of L.A.'s Normandie Club, is the creator of this not-too-sweet lemonade for grown-ups. She gives the drink a lovely floral flavor with a simple chamomile tea syrup that would also be delicious with club soda.

4 oz. water
2 oz. fresh lemon juice
1½ oz. Chamomile Tea Syrup (below)
   Ice
1 lemon wheel and chamomile flowers (optional), for garnish

In a cocktail shaker, combine the water, lemon juice and Chamomile Tea Syrup. Fill the shaker with ice and shake well. Strain into a chilled, ice-filled wineglass and garnish with the lemon wheel and chamomile flowers. —*Devon Tarby*

CHAMOMILE TEA SYRUP
In a small saucepan, bring 4 oz. water to a boil. Off the heat, steep 2 chamomile tea bags in the water for 5 minutes. Add ½ cup sugar and stir until dissolved. Discard the tea bags. Let the syrup cool, pour into a jar and refrigerate for up to 3 weeks. Makes about 5 oz. —*DT*

● STRONG   ● SWEET   ● TART   ● BITTER   ● FRUITY   ● HERBAL   ● SMOKY   ● SPICY

COCO LOCO

WISE GUY

WISE GUY

MAKES **1 drink**

BASE **Pineapple juice**

"Verjus is an incredible ingredient and is sadly underutilized behind the bar," says Lacy Hawkins, bartender at The NoMad in New York City. Verjus, the juice of unripened grapes, gives this julep-style mock-tail a nuanced tanginess.

4 sage leaves, plus 1 sprig for garnish
¼ oz. Jalapeño Agave Syrup (below)
1½ oz. fresh pineapple juice
1 oz. verjus (available at specialty food stores)
½ oz. fresh lime juice
Pinch of kosher salt
Ice cubes, plus crushed ice (p. 23) for serving
Pinch of Aleppo pepper, for garnish

In a cocktail shaker, lightly muddle the 4 sage leaves with the Jalapeño Agave Syrup. Add the pineapple juice, verjus, lime juice and salt. Fill the shaker with ice cubes and shake well. Fine-strain (p. 23) into a chilled, crushed ice–filled julep cup and garnish with the sage sprig and Aleppo pepper. —*Lacy Hawkins*

JALAPEÑO AGAVE SYRUP

In a heatproof measuring cup, stir 4 oz. agave syrup into 2 oz. hot water until combined. Stir in ½ chopped unseeded jalapeño and let steep for 5 minutes. Strain the syrup into a heatproof jar, let cool and refrigerate for up to 2 weeks. Makes about 5 oz. —*LH*

LITTLE PRINCE

MAKES **1 drink**

BASE **Yerba mate soda**

Maxwell Britten created this crisp mocktail with William Elliot of Maison Premiere in Brooklyn. The base is Club-Mate, a low-sugar energy soda made from yerba mate. The soda, guzzled by German hackers to fuel late-night coding sessions, is gaining cult status in the US.

5 mint leaves, plus more for garnish
½ oz. Rich Simple Syrup (p. 25)
1¼ oz. fresh lime juice
    Ice
6 oz. Club-Mate (available at health clubs)
    Pinch of finely grated lime zest, for garnish

In a cocktail shaker, combine the 5 mint leaves, Rich Simple Syrup and lime juice. Fill the shaker with ice and shake well. Strain into a chilled, ice-filled collins glass and stir in the Club-Mate. Garnish with mint leaves and lime zest. —*Maxwell Britten and William Elliot*

●●●●●●●●●

LA ISLA DEL SOL

MAKES **1 drink**

BASE **Pineapple juice**

"This drink is great for times when you're keeping it light but want the fuller flavor of a real cocktail," says Sean Kenyon of Williams & Graham in Denver.

(Most bitters are alcohol-based. For a completely nonalcoholic cocktail, leave them out.)

1 cardamom pod
3 oz. fresh pineapple juice
½ oz. fresh lemon juice
½ oz. Rich Simple Syrup (p. 25)
1 large egg white
3 dashes of aromatic bitters, preferably Fee Brothers
    Ice
1 pineapple wedge, for garnish

In a cocktail shaker, muddle the cardamom pod. Add the pineapple juice, lemon juice, Rich Simple Syrup, egg white and 2 dashes of the bitters and shake vigorously. Fill the shaker with ice and shake again. Strain into a chilled coupe. Dot with a line of bitters and garnish with the pineapple wedge. —*Sean Kenyon*

THE SONG DYNASTY

MAKES **1 drink**

BASE **Grapefruit juice**

To give this drink a fluffy head of foam, New York City bartender Lacy Hawkins stops straining the ingredients into the glass just below the rim. She then lets the drink rest for 10 seconds before continuing to strain.

2 oz. chilled club soda
3 oz. fresh grapefruit juice
1 oz. heavy cream
1 oz. Honey Syrup (p. 25)
½ oz. Spicy Ginger Syrup (below)
½ tsp. matcha green tea powder
  Ice

Pour the club soda into a chilled fizz glass. In a cocktail shaker, combine the grapefruit juice, cream, Honey Syrup, Spicy Ginger Syrup and matcha powder. Fill the shaker with ice and shake well. Fine-strain (p. 23) into the fizz glass.
—Lacy Hawkins

SPICY GINGER SYRUP

In a jar, combine 2 oz. fresh ginger juice (from two 3-inch pieces) with ¼ cup sugar. Cover and shake until the sugar dissolves. Refrigerate for up to 2 weeks. Makes about 3 oz. —LH

● STRONG ● SWEET ● TART ● BITTER ● FRUITY ● HERBAL ● SMOKY ● SPICY

PETTY CASH
GUACAMOLE
P. 185

BAR
FOOD

PALOMA
P. 143

SPICY LIME LEAF BEER NUTS

MAKES **6 cups**

TIME **30 min**

Andy Ricker, chef and owner of the Pok Pok restaurants in New York, L.A. and Portland, Oregon, tosses crisp, fried kaffir lime leaves into his spiced nut mix–an example of Thai drinking snacks called kap klaem.

1 cup peanut oil, for frying
10 large fresh kaffir lime leaves (see Note)
8 small dried red chiles
6 cups raw peanuts (2 lbs.)
1 Tbsp. kosher salt
4 large garlic cloves, minced

1. In a very large skillet, heat the peanut oil. Add the lime leaves and chiles and fry over moderate heat until the lime leaves are crisp and the chiles turn deep red, about 1 minute. Using a slotted spoon, transfer the lime leaves and chiles to paper towels to drain.

2. Add the peanuts to the skillet and stir-fry over moderate heat until golden brown, about 10 minutes. Using a slotted spoon, transfer the peanuts to paper towels to drain. Transfer the hot peanuts to a bowl and toss with the salt.

3. Add the garlic to the skillet and fry over moderate heat until golden, about 2 minutes. Using a slotted spoon or fine-mesh skimmer, transfer the garlic to paper towels and pat dry.

4. Using your hands, finely crush the lime leaves and chiles over the peanuts. Add the garlic and toss to combine. Transfer the peanuts to small bowls and serve warm or at room temperature. —*Andy Ricker*

Note It is important to use fresh (not dried) kaffir lime leaves here. They are available at Asian supermarkets; if sold frozen, defrost before using.

Make Ahead The peanuts can be stored in an airtight container for up to 1 week.

CHICKEN CRISPS

TIME **Active 30 min**
Total 1 hr 20 min

Crispy chicken skins rival fried pork rinds. At Yusho in Chicago, chef Matthias Merges bakes them until crackly, then tops them with sweet and salty seasonings.

½ **cup vegetable oil**
5 **garlic cloves, very thinly sliced**
¾ **lb. chicken skin in large pieces**
   (from 3 to 4 chickens), excess fat removed
   Kosher salt and togarashi (Japanese seasoning mix)
   Whole-grain mustard, for brushing
   Honey, for drizzling
   Finely grated lime zest, for garnish

1. Preheat the oven to 375° and line 2 baking sheets with parchment paper. In a small saucepan, combine the vegetable oil with the sliced garlic and cook over moderate heat, stirring often, until the garlic is golden and crisp, about 8 minutes. Using a slotted spoon, transfer the garlic chips to paper towels to drain.

2. Spread out the chicken skin in a single layer on the prepared baking sheets and season lightly with salt and togarashi. Top the chicken skin with another sheet of parchment paper and another baking sheet to weigh it down. Bake for 40 to 50 minutes, until the skins are golden and crisp; rotate the baking sheets from front to back and top to bottom halfway through baking.

3. Transfer the crispy chicken skins to paper towels to drain. Lightly brush with whole-grain mustard and transfer to a serving bowl. Drizzle lightly with honey, garnish with the garlic chips and lime zest and serve. —*Matthias Merges*

Make Ahead The crispy chicken skins and garlic chips can be kept at room temperature for up to 3 hours. Brush with mustard and drizzle with honey before serving.

TOSTONES WITH CHILE VINEGAR

SERVES **6**

TIME **45 min**

The secret to L.A. chef Roy Choi's tasty tostones–fried plantains–is the chile vinegar he sprinkles on top. In the movie *Chef,* Jon Favreau's character hawks these tostones from his Cuban-inspired food truck. Choi, a food truck pioneer and technical consultant to *Chef,* created the recipe specifically for the film.

½ cup unseasoned rice vinegar
1 garlic clove, crushed
4 red jalapeños or Fresno chiles— stemmed, seeded and chopped
2 Thai chiles, stemmed
Kosher salt
Vegetable oil, for frying
4 large green plantains, peeled and sliced ½ inch thick

1. In a blender, puree the vinegar, garlic, jalapeños and Thai chiles until smooth. Transfer the chile vinegar to a bowl and season with salt.

2. In a saucepan, heat 2 inches of vegetable oil to 350°. Working in batches, fry the plantains just until pale golden, 6 minutes. Using a slotted spoon, transfer the plantains to a paper towel–lined baking sheet. Using a meat pounder or ceramic mug, flatten the plantain slices until they're ¼ inch thick.

3. Reheat the oil to 375°. Working in batches, fry the plantains until crisp, 5 minutes. Drain on paper towels and season with salt. Serve with the chile vinegar. —*Roy Choi*

Make Ahead The chile vinegar can be refrigerated for up to 1 week.

PETTY CASH GUACAMOLE

The salty crunch of pepitas (hulled pumpkin seeds) makes this creamy, spicy guacamole from L.A.'s Petty Cash taqueria especially good.

📷 p. 178

- 2 **small ripe Hass avocados—peeled, pitted and cut into large chunks**
- 2 **Tbsp. fresh lime juice**
- 2 **Tbsp. finely chopped cilantro**
- 1 **Tbsp. roasted pepitas, chopped**
- 1 **Tbsp. chopped tomato**
- ½ **serrano chile, minced**
- 1 **tsp. finely chopped red onion**
  Kosher salt

In a blender, combine the avocados and lime juice and puree until smooth. Transfer the puree to a small bowl. Stir in the remaining ingredients, season with salt and serve. —*Walter Manzke*

OYSTERS ON THE HALF SHELL WITH CEVICHE TOPPING

MAKES **1 dozen oysters**

TIME **30 min**

Dylan Fultineer, the chef at Rappahannock in Richmond, Virginia, is always dreaming up new ways to show off Chesapeake Bay oysters. This is one of his favorites: The combination of raw seafood and a tangy cilantro-chile topping evokes ceviche.

1 tsp. coriander seeds

¼ cup finely diced peeled Asian pear

¼ cup peeled, seeded and finely diced cucumber

1 serrano chile, seeded and minced

1 Tbsp. minced cilantro

1 Tbsp. fresh lime juice

1 tsp. minced candied ginger

1 tsp. Asian fish sauce

1 tsp. extra-virgin olive oil

Kosher salt and pepper

12 freshly shucked oysters on the half shell, such as Rappahannocks

1. In a small skillet, toast the coriander seeds over moderate heat until fragrant, about 2 minutes. Let cool, then coarsely crush the seeds in a mortar. In a small bowl, mix the crushed coriander with all of the remaining ingredients except the oysters.

2. Arrange the oysters on crushed ice. Spoon some of the topping on each one and serve right away, passing additional topping at the table.
—*Dylan Fultineer*

MINTY PEAS + BACON ON TOAST

Chef Greg Vernick is a toast expert: He serves several kinds as appetizers at Vernick Food & Drink in Philadelphia. Here, he purees frozen peas with mint and butter to spread on thick slices of sourdough bread with bacon on top. The toasts soak up the bacon fat in the oven.

1 cup frozen peas, thawed

2 Tbsp. unsalted butter, softened

2 Tbsp. cream cheese, softened

¼ cup lightly packed mint leaves, plus chopped mint for garnish

Kosher salt and cayenne pepper

Four ½-inch-thick slices of sourdough bread

Extra-virgin olive oil, preferably fruity, for brushing and garnish

12 thin bacon slices (6 oz.)

1. Preheat the oven to 400°. In a food processor, combine the peas with the butter, cream cheese and ¼ cup of mint. Pulse until nearly smooth; season the pea butter with salt and cayenne.

2. Brush the bread with olive oil and arrange the slices on a rimmed baking sheet. Toast the bread in the oven for about 8 minutes, turning once, until lightly golden but still chewy in the center. Transfer the toasts to a work surface; leave the oven on.

3. Spread each toast with about ¼ cup of the pea butter and top with 3 slices of bacon. Arrange the toasts on the baking sheet and bake for about 10 minutes, until the bacon just starts to render. Turn on the broiler and broil the toasts 6 inches from the heat for about 3 minutes, until the bacon starts to brown. Garnish the toasts with olive oil and chopped mint and serve warm.

—Greg Vernick

CHIPOTLE CHICKEN TACOS

190 BAR FOOD

SERVES **4**

TIME **Active 30 min**
Total 1 hr 15 min

Alex Stupak is the chef and owner of Manhattan's Empellón Taqueria and co-author of *Tacos: Recipes and Provocations*. For the recipe here, he roasts and shreds juicy chicken thighs, then tosses the meat in a smoky tomato sauce kicked up with chipotle chiles.

8 **chicken thighs (3 lbs.)**
2 **Tbsp. vegetable oil,**
  plus more for brushing
  Kosher salt and pepper
½ **medium white onion, minced, plus more**
  for serving
2 **jalapeños—stemmed, seeded and minced**
2 **Tbsp. minced chipotle chiles plus 3 Tbsp.**
  adobo sauce from the can or jar
4 **plum tomatoes, finely chopped**
  Warm corn tortillas, cilantro leaves, sour
  cream and lime wedges, for serving

1. Preheat the oven to 350°. On a large rimmed baking sheet, brush the chicken with vegetable oil and season with salt and pepper. Bake for about 45 minutes, until an instant-read thermometer inserted in the largest piece registers 165°. Let cool, then shred the meat; discard the skin and bones.

2. In a large skillet, heat the 2 tablespoons of vegetable oil until shimmering. Add the ½ onion, the jalapeños and a generous pinch of salt and cook over moderate heat, stirring occasionally, until just softened, about 5 minutes. Add the chipotles and adobo sauce and cook for 2 minutes. Add the tomatoes and cook until they have softened and any liquid has evaporated, about 7 minutes. Stir in the shredded chicken and cook until hot, about 3 minutes. Season with salt and pepper.

3. Spoon the chicken into warm corn tortillas and serve with cilantro, sour cream, lime wedges and minced onion. —*Alex Stupak*

CAMBODIAN RED CURRY CHICKEN WINGS

SERVES **4 to 6**

TIME **1 hr**

Boldly flavored and nicely spiced, these Cambodia-inspired wings from Louisville chef Edward Lee require a pile of napkins for wiping the delicious red curry coconut sauce off your fingers.

3 Tbsp. canola oil

2 lbs. chicken wings, tips discarded

2 shallots, minced

4 garlic cloves, minced

2 lemongrass stalks, tender white inner bulbs only, finely chopped

2 Tbsp. minced fresh ginger

2 small dried chiles de árbol, stems discarded

2 Tbsp. soy sauce

1 Tbsp. Asian fish sauce

1 tsp. ground cumin

1 tsp. ground coriander

½ tsp. paprika

½ tsp. freshly grated nutmeg

½ tsp. ground turmeric

1 cup unsweetened coconut milk

Kosher salt

Lime wedges, for serving

1. In a large skillet, heat 2 tablespoons of the oil. Working in 2 batches, cook the wings over moderate heat, turning, until golden all over. Transfer to a paper towel–lined plate to drain.

2. Add the remaining 1 tablespoon of oil to the skillet with the shallots, garlic, lemongrass and ginger; cook over low heat, stirring, until softened, 3 minutes. Stir in the chiles, soy sauce, fish sauce, cumin, coriander, paprika, nutmeg and turmeric and cook until fragrant, 3 minutes. Stir in the coconut milk. Transfer to a blender and puree the sauce.

3. Return the sauce to the skillet. Add the chicken and toss to coat. Cover and cook over low heat until cooked through, 10 minutes. Uncover and cook, stirring, until the sauce is thick, 5 minutes. Season with salt and serve with lime wedges.
—*Edward Lee*

RED CABBAGE + FRIED MORTADELLA OKONOMIYAKI

SERVES **4**

TIME **45 min**

In Japan, over-imbibers look to sober up with okonomiyaki, savory pancakes filled with all kinds of vegetables, meats and seafood. Jonathan Brooks, chef at Milktooth in Indianapolis, makes a deliciously inauthentic version loaded with red cabbage, mortadella and chewy udon noodles and topped with a fried egg. He adds an extra umami boost with furikake, a Japanese seasoning mix that includes seaweed, sesame seeds and dried bonito.

4 oz. fresh or frozen udon noodles

2 slices of bacon

3 large eggs

¾ cup prepared dashi or chicken broth

¾ cup all-purpose flour

½ tsp. kosher salt

2 Tbsp. unsalted butter

¼ lb. mortadella, diced

¾ cup finely shredded red cabbage

2 Tbsp. shredded carrot

Kewpie mayonnaise, Sriracha, hoisin sauce, sliced scallions and furikake, for serving

1. In a saucepan of boiling water, cook the udon until tender, 1 minute. Drain, then cut in half.

2. Preheat the oven to 350°. In a 10-inch ovenproof nonstick skillet, cook the bacon over moderately high heat until crisp, 5 minutes. Drain on paper towels, then coarsely chop.

3. In a bowl, beat 2 eggs with the dashi. Whisk in the flour and salt just until a batter forms. In the skillet, melt 1½ tablespoons of the butter. Add the mortadella and stir-fry over moderately high heat until lightly browned, 2 minutes. Add the cabbage and carrot and stir-fry until just wilted, 1 minute. Stir in the udon and pour the batter into the skillet. Cook until the okonomiyaki is browned on the bottom and set around the edge, 6 minutes. Transfer to the oven and bake for about 7 minutes, until cooked through.

4. In a skillet, melt the remaining butter. Fry the remaining egg over moderate heat until the white is firm and the yolk is runny, 3 to 5 minutes.

5. Invert the okonomiyaki onto a platter. Top with the egg and bacon. Drizzle with Kewpie, Sriracha and hoisin, garnish with scallions and furikake and serve. —*Jonathan Brooks*

MEXICAN AVOCADO BURGERS

MAKES **4 burgers**

TIME **Active 20 min
Total 2 hr 20 min**

In New York City, chef April Bloomfield is unofficially known as the burger goddess. At her new spot, Salvation Burger, she makes burgers with a mix of freshly ground meats. This one gets a hit of flavor from the spice blend that's sprinkled on the meat as it cooks.

Note Ground skirt steak can replace the ground brisket, the ground short rib or both.

6 oz. ground brisket (see Note)
6 oz. ground short rib
6 oz. ground bottom round
6 oz. ground chuck
1½ tsp. ground coriander
1½ tsp. ancho chile powder
¾ tsp. ground cumin
¾ tsp. sweet smoked paprika
¾ tsp. ground oregano
¾ tsp. chipotle chile powder
Kosher salt
8 oz. queso fresco, crumbled
4 hamburger buns, split and toasted
3 Tbsp. Mexican crema or sour cream
1 large avocado—peeled, pitted and sliced
Thinly sliced red onion and cilantro leaves, for serving

1. In a bowl, combine the ground meats, mixing gently with your hands. Divide the meat into 4 pieces and gently shape each into a ¾-inch-thick patty. Set the burgers on a baking sheet and refrigerate until firm, at least 2 hours.

2. In a small bowl, whisk the ground coriander with the ancho powder, cumin, smoked paprika, oregano and chipotle powder to combine.

3. Light a grill or heat a grill pan. Generously season the burgers on both sides with salt. Grill over high heat until browned on the bottom, about 3 minutes. Flip and top each burger with 1 teaspoon of the spice blend; reserve the remaining spice blend for another use. Grill the burgers until browned outside and medium-rare within. Transfer to a rack, top with the queso fresco and let rest for 3 minutes. Spread the toasted buns with the crema. Set the burgers on the buns, top with the avocado, red onion and cilantro and serve. —*April Bloomfield*

TOP 50 NEW BARS

East Coast

BOSTON AREA

The Baldwin Bar

Ran Duan (p. 219) serves singular cocktails at his bar in the Sichuan Garden II restaurant inside the 17th-century Baldwin Mansion. Upstairs at the mansion is a new library-style lounge where Duan mixes stiff drinks like Rock Beats Scissors, with rye, Cynar, China-China liqueur and clove bitters. *2 Alfred St., Woburn; 781-935-8488; thebaldwinbar.com.*

Yvonne's

This modern supper club combines grandeur with quirkiness, and the cocktails follow suit. Guests can sip drinks like Bairdley Legal (mezcal, Cynar, passion fruit and grapefruit soda) at a beautiful mahogany bar that was carved in 1886. *2 Winter Place, Boston; 617-267-0047; yvonnes boston.com.*

NEW YORK CITY

Bar Sardine

This compact neighborhood bar in the West Village serves inspired drinks by Brian Bartels. These include a playful selection of Bloody Mary riffs (featuring ingredients like ramen broth, dill-infused vodka and shishito) and barrel-aged cocktails. *183 W. 10th St., Manhattan; 646-360-3705; barsardinenyc.com.*

Goto

At his tiny, refined izakaya, Kenta Goto (p. 219) gives cocktails a Japanese spin, such as the elegant Sakura Martini, garnished with a cherry blossom. The complex drinks are excellent with the bar's thoughtful small plates, among them pan-sized okonomiyaki (savory pancakes). *245 Eldridge St., Manhattan; 212-475-4411; bargoto.com.*

Leyenda

Ivy Mix (p. 221) gives her cocktails unexpected Latin flair: Take, for instance, Feelings Catcher, with Spanish brandy and guava syrup (p. 102). The drinks pair perfectly with chef Sue Torres's pan-Latin menu. *221 Smith St., Brooklyn; 347-987-3260; leyendabk.com.*

Mace

The spice-oriented drinks here, from Nico de Soto (p. 219; portrait, p. 200), straddle the line between daring and refined. His penchant for unconventional combinations is on display in cocktails like Mustard Seed, with black mustard seed–infused Suze. *649 E. Ninth St., Manhattan; no phone; macenewyork.com.*

Mother of Pearl

Jane Danger (p. 218) mixes outrageously fun tiki drinks behind the bar here. Try the highly Instagrammable Imperial Bulldog (p. 108), with aquavit, cachaça, lime juice and pineapple juice, garnished with an entire bottle of Underberg bitters upside down in the glass. *95 Avenue A, Manhattan; 212-614-6818; motherofpearlnyc.com.*

THE BALDWIN BAR,
BOSTON

Nitecap

At this dark, moody cocktail lounge downstairs from Schapiro's restaurant, co-owner Natasha David (p. 218) serves a variety of drinks with cheeky style, from refreshing spritzes to boozy punches. *120 Rivington St., Manhattan; 212-466-3361; nitecapnyc.com.*

The NoMad Bar

This bi-level bar evokes glamorous old New York. Bar director Leo Robitschek and bartender Lacy Hawkins (p. 220) offer innovative cocktails like a big-batch whiskey sour in a gargantuan spigot jar that serves 12. *10 W. 28th St., Manhattan; 347-472-5660; thenomad hotel.com.*

Roof at Park South

The bottle service scene at many New York City rooftop bars can be off-putting. This laid-back bar, on the other hand, offers views of the city's skyline without the attitude. Bar director Ted Kilpatrick mixes unique cocktails like Daiquiri Por Mi Amante, with strawberry-infused five-year rum, lemon, Tabasco and more strawberry. *125 E. 27th St., Manhattan; 212-204-5222; roofatparksouth.com.*

Seamstress

Pamela Wiznitzer (p. 222) showcases her knowledge of classic drinks at this cocktail bar that feels like an elegant (yet unstuffy) hunting lodge. The menu lists 50 classics in addition to house drinks like Mortimer & Mauve (rye and chai vermouth). *339 E. 75th St., Manhattan; 212-288-8033; seamstressny.com.*

PHILADELPHIA

Charlie Was a Sinner

The plant-based (a.k.a. vegan) menu means that cocktails are largely fruit-, vegetable- and herb-based, sweetened with honey alternatives and sometimes infused with farro or tobacco. The Trans-Siberian, for example, is made with vodka, Sauvignon Blanc, green tea, nectarine, vinegar and basil. *131 S. 13th St.; 267-758-5372; charliewasasinner.com.*

WASHINGTON, DC

Dram & Grain

This speakeasy-style bar has three seatings a night. The cocktail menu rotates quarterly; past offerings have included the Jalisco Manzana, with Don Julio añejo tequila and house-made Braeburn apple soda. *2007 18th St. NW; 202-607-1572; facebook .com/DramandGrain.*

The Partisan

The bar at this meat-centric restaurant features novel cocktails by Jeff Faile. The Fernet Ice Cream Float, a favorite, is made with ginger beer, lime zest, Fernet-Branca ice cream and ginger molasses cookies. There are also 25 wines and four spirits on tap plus funky sour beers to drink with one of the impressive charcuterie plates. *709 D St. NW; 202-524-5322; thepartisandc.com.*

GREENRIVER,
CHICAGO

Midwest

DETROIT

Wright & Co.
The centerpiece of this restaurant, built in a ballroom–turned–jewelry shop, is the endless white marble bar top. Craft cocktails include the tequila-based Pear Trap, with pear brandy, salted pear syrup and Zucca amaro. *1500 Woodward Ave., 2nd Fl.; 313-962-7711; wrightdetroit.com.*

INDIANAPOLIS

Libertine Liquor Bar
The drinks at this downstairs space are divided into two categories: Light and Refreshing, and Boozy and Stirred. In the first category is Cinnamon Toast Punch, a playful spiced-rum punch by bartender Ryan Puckett (p. 221) sweetened with cereal-infused buttermilk and pineapple. *608 Massachusetts Ave.; 317-631-3333; libertineindy.com.*

CHICAGO

Celeste
Celeste pays homage to the spirit of innovation celebrated by the 1893 Chicago World's Fair. Drinks such as Cold Buttered Rum with Angostura bitters and nutmeg are served in a modern and refined barroom. *111 W. Hubbard St.; 312-828-9000; celestechicago.com.*

GreenRiver
Famed restaurateur Danny Meyer's restaurant and bar has an outdoor terrace with a stunning view and an extensive drinks selection from Sean Muldoon and Jack McGarry (of The Dead Rabbit in New York City). Whiskey-focused drinks inspired by historical and cultural figures highlight Chicago's Irish-American roots. *259 E. Erie, 18th Fl.; 312-337-0101; greenriver chi.com.*

Milk Room
This reservations-only "micro bar" seats eight people at a time, ensuring that each guest's experience is highly personalized. Its focus on rare liquors (past bottles

have included a 1958 Campari) means that the menu constantly rotates as bottles run out. *12 S. Michigan Ave., 2nd Fl.; 312-792-3515; milkroom chicago.com.*

MILWAUKEE

Goodkind

At this Bay View restaurant, bartender Katherine Rose collaborates with the chefs to design perfect food-and-cocktail pairings. One to try: smoked whitefish pâté with the Light as a Feather (two kinds of gin, Lillet, spruce and mint syrup and lime Pernod). *2457 S. Wentworth Ave.; 414-763-4706; goodkindbayview.com.*

MINNEAPOLIS

Constantine

Stained glass and 160 candles give this subterranean bar a dramatic look, and its cocktails embrace the theatrical, too. Barman Jesse Held (p. 220) focuses on novelty in his drinks, experimenting with infusions and even creating an "ice program" with different styles and flavors.

1115 Second Ave. S.; 612-886-1297; constantinempls.com.

Coup d'Etat

This vast, 9,000-square-foot restaurant and bar consists of several dining rooms and upper- and lower-level patios. The cocktail menu features original creations as well as reinvented classics like the Smoked Manhattan. *2923 Girard Ave. S.; 612-354-3575; coupdetat mpls.com.*

South

LOUISVILLE

Galaxie

With kitschy neon signs and hipster decor, Galaxie is a relaxed space in which to embrace your inner Star Wars nerd. Its street food–inspired menu offers fries "Vader-style" (curry cheese sauce and pickled carrot) and flatbread tacos called "wakatakas." Cocktails include the Storm Trooper (rum, allspice and ginger beer) and margaritas by the pitcher. *732 E. Market St.; 502-690-6595; galaxiebar.com.*

Le Sel

The downstairs lounge of this sophisticated restaurant serves drinks that are as refined as the New French menu. Cocktails lean toward French spirits, like the green Chartreuse-based Mad Priest and Le Sazerac, made with Cognac as well as the traditional rye whiskey. *1922 Adelicia St.; 615-490-8550; lesel nashville.com.*

DURHAM, NORTH CAROLINA

The Durham

The Durham Hotel's rooftop bar offers incredible views of the city and a refreshing cocktail menu created by local star chef Andrea Reusing. Try the El Rosario (cachaça, Fernet-Branca, honey, mint and black pepper) with one of the small plates or a selection from the seasonal raw bar. *315 E. Chapel Hill St.; 919-768-8831; thedurham.com.*

BALISE,
NEW ORLEANS

CHARLESTON, SOUTH CAROLINA

Minero

The decidedly Mexican-inspired cocktail menu has the requisite margarita and sangria, but also less expected creations like El Espectro: rum, chile, pineapple and lemon oleo-saccharum. All drinks pair well with the restaurant's stellar tacos. *153B E. Bay St.; 843-789-2241; minerorestaurant.com.*

ATLANTA

Ticonderoga Club

This quirky tavern inside the buzzy Krog Street Market is the brainchild of bar impresarios Greg Best and Paul Calvert. Here they serve intricate Southern-inflected drinks like a sorghum-sweetened Cognac sour alongside cans of Schlitz beer. The stellar food menu is simarly high-and low-brow, offering both foie gras and fish sticks. *99 Krog Street NE, Suite W; 404-458-4534; ticonderogaclub.com.*

MIAMI BEACH

The Rum Line

This outdoor lounge excels at rum-centric cocktails, serving 1930s-, '40s- and '50s-style drinks and punches in scorpion bowls. The Green Eyed Bandit is made with cachaça, kale and cucumber juice, jalapeño, lime and sea salt. *1601 Collins Ave.; 305-695-0110; therumline.com.*

NEW ORLEANS

Balise

Chef Justin Devillier updates Creole cuisine; bar director Jesse Carr (formerly of Maison Premiere in Brooklyn) mixes nuanced cocktails like Rollo Raiders–gin and aquavit with Greek yogurt and caraway seeds. *640 Carondelet St.; 504-459-4449; balisenola.com.*

Beachbum Berry's Latitude 29

Renowned tiki authority Jeff "Beachbum" Berry delivers the ultimate tiki experience at this island-themed bar: bamboo-paneled accents, brightly colored, outlandishly garnished cocktails and communal punches. The bar also offers a full menu of updated tiki cuisine, with dishes like a Hawaiian Cuban sandwich on pineapple bread and rumaki reimagined as bacon-wrapped jalapeño with water chestnuts and chicken liver mousse. *321 N. Peters St.; 504-609-3811; latitude29nola.com.*

HOUSTON

Julep

Celebrating the cocktail culture of the South, mixologist Alba Huerta specializes in classics as well as thoughtful riffs, such as the namesake mint julep and a gin-based Oregano Cobbler with sherry gum syrup. The food menu includes oysters, smoked fish deviled eggs and an opulent seafood tower. *1919 Washington Ave.; 713-869-4383; julephouston.com.*

AUSTIN

The Roosevelt Room

The drinks at this sleek yet relaxed lounge are impressive, with a touch of whimsy. Do You Even Lift?, reminiscent of a root beer float, is a complex, nostalgic mix of rum, coffee liqueur, orgeat, cream, root beer, cayenne and cinnamon. *307 W. Fifth St.; 512-494-4094; theroosevelt roomatx.com.*

DALLAS

Midnight Rambler

Tucked away in the basement of the Joule Hotel, this cocktail salon has a glamorous Art Deco style and an array of inventive drinks. Its two bars serve shooters, punches and cocktails like the sour-based Royal Tannenbaum, made with rosemary-and-orange gin, amaro and house-made cranberry soda. *1530 Main St.; 214-261-4601; midnight ramblerbar.com.*

Southwest

LAS VEGAS

Culinary Dropout

The cocktails at this bar with a laid-back vibe and live music are described as Light and Easy, Two-Handed Shandies, Classic Dropouts and Copper-less Mules. Pistols at Dawn (bourbon, ancho chile liqueur, ginger agave and Cabernet) is a creative addition to the last category. *4455 Paradise Rd.; 702-522-8100; culinary dropout.com.*

TUCSON

Sidecar

This modern bar offers three riffs on its namesake drink and a variety of other cocktail categories (Frothy and Shaken, Dark and Stirred). It even has a selection of mocktails, including a fresh juice–and–almond milk concoction called the Orange Almond Julias. *139 S. Eastbourne; 520-795-1819; barsidecar.com.*

West Coast

LOS ANGELES AREA

The Chestnut Club

The elaborate drinks at this dimly lit, industrial-chic lounge are supplemented by Spanish-style gin-and-tonic variations. One such iteration is the Café Paloma, with tequila, Aperol, grapefruit and lime. *1348 14th St., Santa Monica; 310-393-1348; thechestnutclubsm.com.*

Grandpa Johnson's Cocktail Club

A 1920s Hollywood Art Deco–inspired design provides the backdrop for approachable drinks made with unusual ingredients. The Lorraine, for example, includes aloe liqueur, pisco, port, lemon and rose water. *1638 N. Cahuenga Blvd., Hollywood; 323-467-7300.*

Harlowe

The vintage fixtures and classic cocktails here are reminiscent of bars from Hollywood's golden age.

THE WALKER INN,
LOS ANGELES

Star mixologist Dushan Zaric of Employees Only in New York City designed the cocktail program, which includes drinks like the vodka-based Clementine, with Aperol, lemon and mandarin puree. *7321 Santa Monica Blvd., West Hollywood; 323-876-5839; harlowe bar.com.*

The Walker Inn

To enter this luxurious reservations-only cocktail lounge, guests press a button by a secret door at the back of the Normandie Club. Co-owner Devon Tarby (p. 222) serves a tasting menu of themed drinks; past themes have included "Ode to Alice Waters." *3612 W. Sixth St., L.A.; 213-263-2709; thewalkerinnla.com.*

SAN FRANCISCO

Dirty Habit

This restaurant and lounge occupies the former Fifth Floor space at Hotel Palomar. Brian Means mixes cocktails with brown spirits and old whiskeys in gorgeous antique glassware. *12 Fourth St.; 415-348-1555; dirtyhabitsf.com.*

The Perennial

Being sustainable in creative ways is a goal at this bar and restaurant. Many ingredients are grown in the restaurant's garden and on its aquaponic farm. Behind the bar, oft-discarded ingredients find new life: Lemons used to clarify milk cordial get candied with bitters; leftover juice becomes a sherbet for a pisco punch. *59 Ninth St.; 415-500-7788; theperennialsf.com.*

Trou Normand

A spin-off of the stellar Bar Agricole, Thad Vogler's latest venture is open all day, with a serious food menu. The name refers to the French tradition of cleansing the palate between courses with brandy, hence the focus on digestive spirits like Cognac. *140 New Montgomery St.; 415-975-0876; trounormandsf.com.*

PORTLAND, OREGON

Bit House Saloon

With a focus on single-barrel spirits, this old-timey bar offers house versions of classics, plus unique drinks, boiler-makers and cocktails on tap. *727 SE Grand Ave.; 503-954-3913; bithouse saloon.com.*

THE GREEN ROOM,
PORTLAND

The Green Room

Designed as a "waiting room" for the popular Multnomah Whiskey Library, this seat-yourself lounge is a destination in its own right. The short yet sophisticated cocktail menu features drinks like an absinthe frappé. *1124 SW Alder St.; 503-954-1381; mwlpdx.com.*

Victoria Bar

There's a healthy dose of kitsch on the menu at this polished cocktail joint. *Princess Bride*–themed cocktails include The Six Fingered Man (a mix of rum, orange curaçao, orgeat, IPA, lemon) and Inigo Montoya (tequila, cardamaro, ginger, lime, cardamom bitters). *4835 N. Albina Ave.; no phone; victoriapdx.com.*

SEATTLE

Brimmer & Heeltap

This bistro and bar offers unfussy, elegant cocktails like the B&H Mule: shochu, ginger, lemongrass and Sichuan pepper. They all go wonderfully with the restaurant's creative snacks (tapioca puff chips) and family-style dishes (squid fried rice). *425 NW Market St.; 206-420-2534; brimmerandheeltap.com.*

Damn the Weather

This Pioneer Square bar and restaurant is housed in a century-old building with exposed brick and a shimmering 25-foot white oak bar. The Black Cherry Smash, with rye, lemon and shiso, is one example of the bar's bright, complex cocktails. *116 First Ave. S.; no phone; damntheweather.com.*

Good Bar

The menu at this smart, stylish bar in the former Japanese Commercial Bank ranges from classic riffs (like the Darker Stormy, tweaked with a ginger-stout reduction) to the unexpected (the Axl Brose, with Scotch, Drambuie, honey, oatmeal cream, nutmeg and egg yolk). *240 Second Ave. S.; 206-624-2337; goodbarseattle.com.*

Rocky Mountains

DENVER

Occidental

The younger sibling of the Williams & Graham speakeasy has a laid-back, rock 'n' roll vibe, with mix tapes lining the walls and drinks like the Sonic Reducer (bourbon, cranberry liqueur, lemon, honey) from co-owner Sean Kenyon (p. 220). *1950 W. 32nd Ave.; 720-536-8318; occidentalbar.com.*

ASPEN

Jimmy's Bodega

This mezcaleria and seafood restaurant is an offshoot of Jimmy's, Aspen's beloved restaurant and tequila mecca. Cocktails sold by the bottle include the Harvest Manhattan (rye, amaro, maple syrup, pimento bitters) and Goldenrye (rye, sherry, ginger liqueur, lemon). *307 S. Mill St.; 970-710-2182; jimmysbodega.com.*

DRINKS INDEX

DAIQUIRI
P. 137

NEGRONI
P. 149

PDT/CRIF FROZEN
PIÑA COLADA, P. 90

CREDITS

BARWARE GUIDE

BAR TOOLS

pp. 10–11 from left to right: "Mexican Beehive" juicer, "Coco" strainer, "Usagi" heavyweight cobbler shaker, Trident bar spoon, *cocktailkingdom.com*

LOW-PROOF + APERITIF

p. 30 Gold-plated cocktail picks, *cocktailkingdom.com*
p. 36 "Manhattan" large highball, *saint-louis.com*

BRUNCH

p. 41 Seamless paddle mixing glass, *cocktail kingdom.com* **p. 42** "Grip" beer tumbler by Lobmeyr, *tableartonline.com*
p. 48 "Triennale" highball by Lobmeyr, *tableartonline.com*

JUICE-SPIKED

p. 50 Wide-stem cylindrical old-fashioned glass by Sugahara, *dandelionsf.com*

COFFEE + TEA DRINKS

p. 67 "Usagi" heavyweight gold-plated cobbler shaker, *cocktailkingdom.com*

FOUR INGREDIENTS

p. 77 "Harmonie" tumbler, *us.baccarat.com*
p. 78 "Pure" wineglass by Pordamsa, *secure .dandelionsf.com*

FROZEN + SLUSHIE

p. 88 "Fanny" highball tumbler, *williamyeoward crystal.com* **p. 89** "No. 282 Diamondcut" wine tumbler by Lobmeyr, *tableartonline .com*

TIKI + TROPICAL

p. 103 Julep spoon straw, *cocktailkingdom.com;* "Dagny" double old-fashioned glass, *ralphlauren home.com* **p. 104** "Palmyra" tumbler highball, *william yeowardcrystal.com*

HIGH-OCTANE

p. 117 Seamless "Yarai" mixing glass, *cocktail kingdom.com* **p. 125** "Caton" tasting glass, *saint-louis .com* **p. 128** "Hoffman" gold-plated bar spoon, Nick and Nora gold trim glass, *cocktailkingdom.com*

CLASSICS + RIFFS

p. 130 Frosted black glass pitcher by Sugahara, *dandelionsf.com;* "Massena" Champagne coupe, *us.baccarat.com*
p. 131 Square martini glass by Sugahara, *dandelionsf .com;* copper-plated cocktail picks, *cocktailkingdom.com*
p. 141 "Cerdagne" large old-fashioned glass, *saintlouis.com*
p. 147 Antique-style gold-plated Hawthorne strainer, *cocktailkingdom.com*

LARGE-FORMAT

p. 152 "Brenna" martini pitcher, *ralphlaurenhome .com* **p. 158** "Relax" glass by Sugahara, *dandelionsf.com*

MOCKTAILS

p. 174 Silver-plated julep cup, *cocktailkingdom.com*

PHOTOGRAPHS

BAR LEXICON

pp. 16–17 from left to right, courtesy of: Distillerie Branca, Haus Alpenz, Distillerie Branca, thewhiskyexchange.com

pp. 18–19 from left to right, courtesy of: Sazerac Company, Pernod Ricard USA, Distillerie de la Salers, Wölffer Estate

BAR FOOD

p. 181 James Ransom **p. 182** Con Poulos **p. 187** Christina Holmes **p. 188** Lucas Allen **p. 191** Christina Holmes **p. 192** Tara Fisher **p. 195** John Kernick **p. 199** Raul Zelaya **p. 200** Scott Gordon Bleicher **p. 202** Anthony Tahlier **p. 204** Rush Jagoe **p. 207** Katie Wenzel **p. 208** Eddie Hernandez

CONTRIBUTORS

SAM ANDERSON
Anderson is the bar director at Mission Chinese Food and Mission Cantina, both in New York City. His cocktails, often inspired by visits to Chinatown markets, echo the restaurants' innovative cuisine. His coconutty Philippe Khallins mocktail (p. 169) is a clever riff on Thai tom kha gai soup; he even serves the drink in a small soup bowl.

CHAD ARNHOLT As both the bartender at Comstock Saloon in San Francisco and a cofounder of Tin Roof Drink Community, Arnholt focuses on sustainability in mixology. "Feel free to alter the ingredients to include local products," he says. "Get the most out of your neck of the woods!"

JEFF BELL After starting his career as a barback at the legendary PDT in New York City, Bell now runs the show there as general manager, crafting cocktails with bold, exciting flavors. One example: Little Squirt (p. 143), a smoky tequila-and-mezcal concoction with muddled bell pepper and a spice-salt rim.

MAXWELL BRITTEN Best known for his work as bar director at Maison Premiere in Brooklyn, Britten is now the chief brand officer for The Liquor Cabinet, a creative marketing agency. He demonstrates his encyclopedic cocktail knowledge through sophisti-cated, delicious combina-tions like an absinthe-laced eggnog (p. 145).

DEREK BROWN At his sherry and cocktail bar Mocking-bird Hill in Washington, DC, Brown says he's served guests at every level of government, "even the president—but I never tell, without their permission, what they drink." His love for sherry shines in drinks like The Doubting Duck (p. 35).

JULIO CABRERA Before he began running The Regent Cocktail Club in Miami, Cabrera was an agricultural engineer specializing in the growth and harvest of citrus and coffee. Not surprisingly, his drinks incorporate these and other flavors from his native Cuba in brilliant ways; his frozen Bananita Daiquiri (p. 97) blends in coffee beans.

DONNY CLUTTERBUCK
Clutterbuck worked at both dives and swanky bars in Buffalo and New York City before he became the bar manager at Cure in Rochester, New York. He prides himself on his ability to tailor drinks to customers' preferences. He created Desk Job (p. 116) for a guest who wanted a bitter drink without a citrus-based bitter.

JANE DANGER When Danger got her start bartending at 19, her specialties were "pie shots and carrying 15 Bud Lites at once," she says. As the beverage director of Mother of Pearl and Cienfuegos in Manhattan, Danger has a playful style: She serves the passion fruit–inflected Shark Eye (p. 111) in a shark mug.

NATASHA DAVID When she's not behind the bar at Nitecap in New York City, David loves to host dinner parties—hence her talent for mixing home-bartender-friendly, big-batch drinks. The sangria-like Every-thing's Coming Up Rosé (p. 153) is just one of her beautifully complex punches.

BRYAN DAYTON A former competitive ultrarunner, Dayton brings the same dedication to his work as the co-owner and beverage director of Oak at Fourteenth in Boulder, Colorado, and Acorn and Brider in Denver. He shows his ability to create innovative, balanced cocktails with Brunch on the Danube (p. 40), spiked with Zwack and ginger beer.

JOHN DEBARY A veteran bartender at PDT in New York City, deBary is the chief mixologist for *F&W Cocktails 2016* and the bar director of the Momofuku restaurant group. A slushie machine aficionado, he adapted a recipe he created for Fuku in Manhattan for his Blender 163 Iced Tea (p. 90).

JACYARA DE OLIVEIRA Formerly of Sportsman's Club in Chicago, de Oliveira won the 2015 Speed Rack Chicago all-female bartending competition. Her advice to home mixologists: "Measuring is super-important. You don't need as much alcohol in a cocktail as you think you do."

NICO DE SOTO Born in Paris, de Soto has worked in cocktail establishments around the world. At his bar Mace in New York City, he uses unconventional infusions inspired by global cuisines—dill tequila, shiitake agave—to create exceptional drinks.

NICK DETRICH At Cane & Table in New Orleans, Detrich's mixology style is heavily influenced by the city's cocktail history. His Two Mirrors (p. 70), with cold-brew coffee and anisey Herbsaint, is a tribute to the absinthe frappé, a cocktail invented in New Orleans and often imbibed during Mardi Gras parades.

RAN DUAN Though Duan didn't plan on working for the family business, he ended up behind the bar at Sichuan Garden II, his parents' Chinese restaurant in Woburn, Massachusetts. In 2012, Duan opened The Baldwin Bar on the first floor of the restaurant, where he mixes drinks that are "very simple to make, yet with a lot of complexity," such as Father's Advice (p. 111).

ANU ELFORD From a young age, Elford learned the importance of hard work: "My first job was at 13, picking cherries on a farm in Utah starting at 5 a.m.," she says. Elford has since brought her work ethic and considerable talent to Seattle, founding Swig Well, a bartending academy, and launching the bar Rob Roy. Two more bars, No Anchor and Navy Strength, are her latest projects.

LINDSAY FERDINAND As beverage director at Common Quarter in Atlanta, Ferdinand takes cocktails to the next level with unusual DIY shrubs and syrups. For instance, lavender syrup gives the vodka-based Suburban Anxiety (p. 62) a delicate floral flavor.

KENTA GOTO Growing up in Japan, Goto helped at his mother's restaurant, which specialized in okonomiyaki (savory Japanese pancakes). At Bar Goto, his New York City bar, he draws on this experience, serving various okonomiyaki with Japanese-inflected drinks like Matcha Milk Punch (p. 66).

KAREN GRILL Grill is a cocktail consultant for The Bon Vivants and a bartender at Melrose Umbrella Co. in Los Angeles. She believes in unpretentious drinks: "There is something so special about a simple cocktail made with great care that can still blow a guest's mind," she explains. Case in point: her four-ingredient South of Sunset Negroni riff (p. 79).

LACY HAWKINS Though Hawkins started her career in the cocktail industry as a nightclub bouncer, she soon transitioned to a spot behind the bar. Now, she mixes drinks at The NoMad and Clover Club, both in New York City. In her spare time, she enjoys beekeeping.

JESSE HELD At Constantine in Minneapolis, Held's drinks fuse the approach-able and the unusual. In Beyond the Walking Dead (p. 126), he creates his own version of a zombie by supercharging the tiki classic with four kinds of rum, spiced liqueur and a variety of bitters. The result exemplifies his focus on classic technique with creative flair.

BOBBY HEUGEL With Anvil Bar & Refuge, Heugel put Houston on the mixology map and made customers re-appreciate classics by using quality ingredients. He continues to enhance the city's cocktail culture by opening spaces like The Pastry War, a mezcaleria that emphasizes tradition. But he also likes to have fun: He serves his Caribbean Fairy absinthe punch (p. 154) in fresh coconuts.

SEAN HOARD As general manager of Teardrop Cocktail Lounge in Portland, Oregon, Hoard focuses on seasonal ingredients for the constantly rotating drinks menu. He also makes cocktails that can be enjoyed year-round: His boozy, slow-sipping Golden Slumbers (p. 122) includes overproof tequila, Grand Marnier, Cocchi Americano and Suze.

SARA JUSTICE The regional Pennsylvania Dutch cuisine that Justice grew up with inspired her love of food, leading her to a career behind the bar. At The Franklin Bar in Philadelphia, she particularly enjoys interacting with guests. One

of her tips for a cocktail-filled evening? "I serve guests with hiccups three lime wedges doused in sugar and Angostura bitters. I have never seen it fail."

SEAN KENYON A third-generation bartender, Kenyon was 16 when he started working at his family's pub. At his speakeasy Williams & Graham and his bar Occidental, both in Denver, he continues his 30-year bartending career, making an impressive array of both classic and creative cocktails. His St. Henry Punch (p. 156) falls into the latter category, with its refreshing combination of green tea, honeydew juice and ginger liqueur.

CHRIS LANE At the bar at Ramen Shop in Oakland, California, Lane creates cocktails that complement the restaurant's umami-rich dishes. Drinks like Double-Barrel Fizz (p. 138), with cherry gastrique, rye and cinnamon, hit both sweet and savory notes. When he's not behind the bar, Lane works as a freelance illustrator.

MICAH MELTON

One of Melton's first jobs at The Aviary in Chicago was working as the restaurant's "ice chef," making more than 30 different types for the bar program. Now, as the restaurant's beverage director, he brings this same creativity to the cocktail list. The Wasabi Grasshopper (p. 99) is a complex twist on the retro classic, frozen in an ice cream machine with wasabi powder.

IVY MIX

At 19, Mix served her first drink while studying in Guatemala, where she fell in love with tequila and mezcal. As the co-owner and head bartender of Leyenda in Brooklyn, she shows off her extensive knowledge of agave spirits with cocktails like Tia Mia (p. 102), a smoky mezcal mai tai riff. Mix is also a cofounder of Speed Rack, the all-female national cocktail competition.

LINDSAY NADER

Nader is a renowned bartender and co-owner of Juice Saves, a cold-pressed juice bar in San Diego. She is adept at making outstanding juice-based cocktails like Silly Rabbit (p. 55), with fresh carrot and lemon juice, pear brandy, yellow Chartreuse and a spicy ginger syrup.

RYAN PUCKETT

Though Puckett didn't intend to be a bartender (he has a degree in animation), he fell in love with mixology. It happened by chance after stepping behind the bar at the Libertine Liquor Bar in Indianapolis when someone failed to show up for a shift. But his career path, he insists, was preordained: "*Cocktail* was the number one movie in America on the day I was born," he explains.

JESSICA SANDERS

Sanders, co-owner of Drink. Well and Backbeat in Austin, believes in creating drinks that are both meaningful and delicious. "Cocktails with a rich story or ones that are inspired by history, art or poetry," she says, "can be a great way to connect with guests." For instance, Spanish Harlem (p. 127), a boozy and flavorful mix of rum, orange-infused sherry and date syrup, is a nod to Sanders's time living in the New York City neighborhood of the same name.

JACK SCHRAMM

Beyond his degree in food studies, Schramm is passionate about all things culinary: "I once ate a 66-ounce rib eye in one sitting and am surprisingly adept at catching things in my mouth," he says. He brings this same vigor and enthusiasm to the cocktails he crafts at Booker and Dax in New York City. His Bitter's Breakfast (p. 76) is a coffee-and-amaro concoction inspired by the classic Italian combination.

JOAQUÍN SIMÓ

A former deputy editor of *F&W Cocktails,* Simó grew up eating fruits and vegetables from his grandfather's farm in Miami. His appreciation for food eventually transformed into an obsession with cocktails. After working on the opening of the acclaimed Manhattan bar Death & Company, Simó launched Pouring Ribbons, also in Manhattan. There, he mixes drinks like Hagar the Gentle (p. 49), a complex brunch cocktail with hints of anise, caraway and rosemary.

SHANNON SMITH

As the general manager of Porco Lounge and Tiki Room in Cleveland, Smith expertly crafts some of the Midwest's finest tropical cocktails. His style ranges from drinks like Little Plastic Castles (p. 105)—"an ode to the simple classics of tiki"—to the unexpected yet stellar combination of coffee and passion fruit in Dilapidated Beach House (p. 112).

EZRA STAR

After spending several years studying biochemistry, Star turned her scientific sensibilities toward cocktails. At Drink in Boston, she often creates off-the-cuff drinks for guests, including one that became the 1910 (p. 134), a Manhattan riff with Punt e Mes vermouth, mezcal and Cognac.

DEVON TARBY

Inventiveness is key for Tarby, co-owner of The Walker Inn and The Normandie Club in L.A. She likes to think of new ways to enliven standbys: "Our menu changes frequently, with variations of classically structured drinks," she explains. Her Normandie Club Spritz (p. 32), a grapefruit-and-elderflower-inflected take on the classic effervescent cocktail, includes vermouth, tequila, pisco and citrus.

ANDREW VOLK

At Portland Hunt & Alpine Club in Maine, Volk mixes everything from "brown and bitter" cocktails to "classics and riffs." He strives to make "geeky, delicious, accessible, fun" drinks like Norseman (p. 140), with brown butter–washed aquavit; and In Cold Blood (p. 85), a pleasingly bitter cocktail balanced by a thoughtful pinch of salt. "I'm partial to martinis and daiquiris," he says, "but who isn't?"

KYLE LINDEN WEBSTER

At Expatriate in Portland, Oregon, Webster (who owns the bar with his wife, F&W Best New Chef 2009 Naomi Pomeroy) explores unusual flavor combinations. The results: exceptional drinks such as Air Bag (p. 34), a tart, refreshing aperitif made with myrtle berry liqueur. His Sunless Sea (p. 31) balances the flavors of grapefruit and pear with chile liqueur.

PAMELA WIZNITZER

Behind the bar at Seamstress in New York City, Wiznitzer serves sophisticated cocktails with unexpected elements. For instance, Cold in the Shadows (p. 49), a fruity brunch drink with lime juice, raspberry liqueur and honey syrup, gets a bitter twist from Campari and hoppy IPA-style beer.

EMILY YETT

At Herbs & Rye in Las Vegas, Yett slings drinks categorized by the era when they were first created, from the Gothic Age to the Rat Pack Era. Her Golden Spritz (p. 28), which combines the bitter aperitif Salers with vermouth and Prosecco, is a modern twist on the Champagne cocktail, a favorite in the 1930s.

CONVERSION CHART

Measures for spirits and other liquids are given in fluid ounces.

CUP		OUNCE		TBSP		TSP
1 c	=	8 fl oz				
¾ c	=	6 fl oz				
⅔ c	=	5⅓ fl oz				
		5 fl oz	=	10 Tbsp		
½ c	=	4 fl oz				
		3 fl oz	=	6 Tbsp		
⅓ c	=	2⅔ fl oz				
¼ c	=	2 fl oz				
		1 fl oz	=	2 Tbsp		
		½ fl oz	=	1 Tbsp	=	3 tsp
		⅓ fl oz	=	⅔ Tbsp	=	2 tsp
		¼ fl oz	=	½ Tbsp	=	1½ tsp

1 ounce = about 32 dashes
1 dash = 4 to 5 drops

More books from

FOOD&WINE

ANNUAL COOKBOOK
An entire year of FOOD & WINE recipes.

BEST OF THE BEST
The best recipes from the 25 best cookbooks of the year.

WINE GUIDE
Pocket-size guide with more than 1,000 recommendations.